Management: From the Outside Looking In

Becoming a better leader & manager using an "outside" approach

Zachary M. Frace

This book is to provide guidance to readers in a leadership or management career path and may contain personal encounters. Identities and events will remain as confidential as possible.

Visit my website at www.ManagementofHealthcare.com

Written, reviewed, and printed in the United States of America.

This book is dedicated to:

All my past managers and mentors who have allowed me to gain valuable insights that encouraged me to write this book by providing me the theory of utilizing an outside approach to be a successful leader and manager.

Table of Contents

Introduction..1

PART I: Becoming a Better Leader......................3

    Chapter One: Being a Leader.....................7

    Chapter Two: Inspiring & Motivating Others...17

    Chapter Three: Avoid Being a Boss 27

    Chapter Four: Never Stop Learning 37

    Chapter Five: Building Relationships............45

Part II: Becoming a Better Manager.....................55

    Chapter Six: Internal vs. External Hire 57

    Chapter Seven: Communication..................67

    Chapter Eight: Responsibility.....................77

    Chapter Nine: Personal Quality Assurance......85

    Chapter Ten: Social Media and Appreciation....93

Epilogue/Conclusion....................................105

Acknowledgements......................................107

About the Author...109

Introduction

With so many tutorials, blogs, and books out there, I want to personally thank you for taking the time to read my content. I am here to provide guidance for an array of people such as managers, directors, entrepreneurs, students, and anyone that is looking to enhance their leadership skills to get to the next level or touch up on their existing roles.

Many, if not all, books about management and leadership are from those who have been managers for decades or have doctorates and looking to build their portfolio. This book, however, will help guide individuals to take an outside approach in management. What does this mean exactly? It means that many times managers, at any level, lose sight on their employee's perspective of how well they are really managing things. This can oftentimes be resolved by simply stepping back and look at their role and actions as if they are in their employee's shoes.

I have worked as a manager and I do consider myself a strong leader, but I am by no means an expert in management. What I do have is my MBA in healthcare administration, a bachelor's degree in medical imaging and certified by the American Registry of Radiologic Technologists in both radiography and CT scan. I have worked and shadowed thirteen different companies in the past ten years and have experienced many management styles that have ultimately led me to writing this book.

Some of the information that I am presenting may seem elementary or ridiculous that it needs to be mentioned, however this is written on many past experiences and information from others I have gathered. I am presenting information in this book is to help redirect your mindset in your current or future management position and hopefully stop preventable issues from occurring. If you feel that your employees are not respecting you or that you are not getting to your desired goal, then this is the book for you! Start to lead your department in a more effective way and have your department stand out with your improved managerial skills.

PART I: Becoming A Better Leader

This part of the book will dive into developing the essential skills that it takes to become a successful leader. These skills are often adapted by past experiences and management styles on different hierarchy levels. It will cover the fundamentals from basic leadership skills all the way to a professional leader in a professional role. I want to stress the importance of leadership by inspiring and motivating others to become leaders, avoiding the title of being the "boss", the importance of continuing education, and building relationships.

Leadership is an important trait that many possess but may not utilize to their maximum potential. How often do you encounter an employee who is well-knowledgeable, punctual, sets an example for others, and is always relied on? You probably know a handful. How many of these employees make an excuse for not trying to achieve more than they are capable of because of the classic excuses such as: "I am not paid to do that", "that's not my job", "I used to care 20 years ago", "management doesn't recognize my efforts, so why bother?", and many other excuses that prevent employees from reaching their fullest potential? These people can still achieve leadership status by correct guidance from other leaders, but most importantly, the manager. Managers share equal responsibility in the success of building upon leaders of their department.

Leaders are not true leaders if they are not willing to allow others to achieve the same or more success than themselves. Inspiring and motivating others is an important factor of leadership qualities because a cruise ship can only be driven by the captain for so long before a pilot or shipmate needs to take over. You need to lead others so you can depend on them when you need them most. As the adage goes, "give a man a fish and you'll feed him for a day, teach him to fish and he will be fed for life". This same is true with leadership. One leader cannot make a huge difference, however, if one leader encourages others to work by the same standards, a difference can and will be made.

There are many misconceptions that managers are bosses. The word "boss" has such a negative connotation that should not be used when speaking of management, unless of course, they are indeed "bossy". Leadership/management can sometimes be bossy and demanding of other employees. Sometimes this bossy behavior may be caused from high pressure situations that they are delegating and may come off as demanding. These incidences are infrequent and often unintended from real leaders. This can come strictly from an alpha mindset in which an individual naturally wants to take direct control of a situation. This differs from a bullying attitude where one thinks they are more superior than others. Bullies often present a demanding and cold behavior towards others. This will be discussed more in chapter 3.

Chapter 4, "Never Stop Learning", will evaluate the many ways leaders are able to continue their education in both a formal and informal manner. Leaders have a natural drive that will cause them to learn the most they can. This drive is to not only improve their knowledge and self-worth, but to utilize this knowledge to better others. There is always something to learn every single day. Even a CEO of a fortune-500 company with a doctorate degree should learn at least one fact, tasks, or skill each day or week. They may be an expert in their respected industry, however they are human and there is always something to learn, even if it is in a different industry that could be beneficial to them one day. For example, Apple Inc. used to be strictly a computer company. Obviously, they turned into one of the largest manufacturers of mobile phones and even expanded into other domains. They grew to such a large scale that they have put a phone in approximately 1 out of every 3 people's hands in the United States. They did not just stop there, they have also developed a partnership with EPIC, an Emergency Health Records system, to integrate their customer's health information into their phones and create one integrated system. Without learning about the medical field, health information technology, and the potential that these two can create, this would never have happened. This is a very important topic that many may overlook and is far more complex than the concept of simply going back to school to continue learning. It has a deeper meaning that we can learn from these types of companies that do not settle, but rather integrate to expand their product line and services. All of this involves a different way of thinking and a very open mindset to be successful both your professional life but also your business you may own or manage.

"Building Relationships", will be the last chapter in this leadership section. This chapter will evaluate the different types of relationships leaders should have with their co-workers and managers to be successful. We will be focusing on building a list of mentors that will provide the support needed to guide you towards a successful career.

"If your actions inspire others to dream more, learn more, do more and become more, you are a leader."

- John Quincy Adams, 6th President of the United States of America.

Chapter One: Being A Leader

Leadership skills cannot be learned overnight. Although it is often an innate trait, it can also be learned through simple observation and the desire to make a positive impact. There is a common misconception that leaders are managers and managers are leaders. Starting now, we are going to separate these two words and treat them as two separate concepts. Look at it this way: John is the manager of fifteen employee and relies heavily on one of his highly engaged employees named Craig. John, the manager, arrives directly to his office in an executive wing, far from the department that he manages and will stay there until lunch time when he checks on his employees. Craig, on the other hand arrives in a punctual manner and analyzes the day to come. He ensures that the department has everything it needs to run smoothly throughout the day. Craig sets a motivational presence that allows others to feel security that the day is well planned and taken care of. Craig is relied on because he allows himself to be a stronger presence in the department than the manager. Great leaders tend to possess ten very similar attributes, which are outlined in Figure 1.1.

10 Attributes of Great Leaders

1.	Transparency	Having someone who is open about possible changes or issues, whether good or bad, is important to employees.

2.	Passion	Someone who is passionate in their role and profession look for ways to grow themselves to better their workplace.
3.	Empathy	Someone who can emphasize with other co-workers is important, which is especially true when it comes to when employees need off.
4.	Open-Minded	When others present new ideas, it is important as a leader to have an open mind about these ideas or changes that are presented to them.
5.	Patient	Not everyone goes at the same pace or delivers quick responses to your ideas. It is important to have patience when in a leadership role.
6.	Integrity	Leaders should be honest, reliable, and someone that others can resort to knowing that they will try their best to accomplish it.
7.	Confidence	When a leader has confidence, it shows. When others notice your lack of confidence, it trickles on them because they view you as a leader and when the leader looks unsure, so are they.

8.	Excellent Communication	This is a big one. Communication relays information. Without communication employees are not kept in the look and you may be viewed as if you are hiding something important.
9.	Delegation	When busy, it is important to have delegation skills or you may have the same task being completed by different people. Give everyone a purposeful task or job that will efficiently complete your end goal.
10.	Creativity	Be creative in how you deliver new ideas. Good ideas stem from creativity. Leaders are expected to be creative to solve problems because not every problem can be found in a textbook or Google.

Figure 1.1

Managers are typically worried about the bigger picture of the department and often lose sight of improving the quality of the department or business. Leaders on the other hand are not usually the ones to make big decisions and therefore allows them the flexibility to brainstorm and collaborate with other co-workers about any current or future projects or ideas that could improve the efficiency and morale of the department. To become a successful manager, one must master being a successful leader and not let go of those leadership qualities once they step into a managerial role. Although leadership qualities often get lost when a leader becomes a manager, it is important to reflect on how they achieved their success so they can carry that over with them as a manager and inspire leaders who yearn the same path of leadership.

Leaders are strongly involved within their department and invested in their employee's wellbeing. The try their best to look for innovative solutions to common problems that they or their coworker's encounter. Problems and issues are bound to happen in the workplace, however recurring problems can be problematic in the long run. As a leader, having a form of methodology to fix problems is important to prevent them from happening in the future. The method that I like to use is what I call the 2x2 method. If a small issue occurs two or more times within two days, or larger issues occur two or more times in two weeks, then there is an issue that needs to be fixed. An example of a small issue using the 2x2 method could be an employee forgetting to restock the department two days in a row when it is part of their responsibility. This is not a huge deal but since it happened more than once there may be something preventing this employee from getting their job done. A leader will look for a simple solution such as a simple reminder for the employee the next day they work.

A bigger issue using the 2x2 method may be an x-ray technologist x-raying the wrong patient twice within two weeks. Due to radiation protection, this is a huge deal and the technologist should be disciplined by the manager. However, as a leader you should look for innovative solutions to prevent this from happening again such as a checklist each employee needs to complete before performing an exam as a reminder and to prevent this mistake from happening again. The biggest take of this is not to micromanage but to be mindful and attentive of how others are performing or mistakes that are being made.

Leaders are the gatekeepers for their co-workers and although they are not always formally responsible for them or decision making, they play a vital role to keep the department or business running smoothly. To be a great leader, you must be able to transform concerns and ideas from an employee's perspective to management. Managers are often displaced and need leaders to explain from an employee's point of view. An example of this would be frequently being short staffed. The manager may not see a huge issue with this because after all, it is saving the company money due to lower labor costs. From a leader and employee's perspective there is a large issue because there is discontent from those who must work just as hard for no incentive. Explaining to the manager, as a leader, would require explaining the concerns of the staff and dissatisfaction that they are having and that it could lead to employees leaving or being disengaged, which leads to lower productivity.

Being a leader takes a type of unique commitment that is far beyond the average employee. There are many types of leaders who utilize either a transformational or transactional leadership approach. A transformational leader is primarily focused on individual's wellbeing that drives them to be more productive and satisfied. A transactional leader focuses on current problems and how to solve them in an orderly fashion. Neither one is better than the other and they both offer unique approaches to problem-solving. Leaders, who have no formal job title and considered equal ranking as their co-workers, are typically preferred to be transitional in nature because they have more commonly shared goals.

Transitional leaders are typically more favored because they are employee-focused, while transactional leaders are primarily concerned for issues that are occurring at the very moment. This type of leader is either a supervisor or a team member who tends to focus on problems that are unrelated to their job description, but they feel the need to fix it right then and there. This can cause tension in the department because the employee is physically and mentally pulled from the department and will not to stop until they figure out the problem at hand because they feel it is their responsibility even if it does not pertain to their duties or job description.

You cannot decide whether you want to be a transitional or transactional leader, it is merely the type of leadership style in which you have developed within. It is not wrong to be one or the other. You may even possess some traits of both, however you can determine your style by asking yourself this question, "are you more concerned for ensuring there is adequate staffing to provide the best patient/customer care and avoid burnout, or are you more concerned about sticking to a strict budget?". If you are worried about the first part, then you are transitional. If you are more worried about the budget, then you can consider yourself transactional. Figure 1.2 will help those who are more visual learners differentiate the two.

Transformational	Transactional
Focuses on the vision.	Focuses on goals.
Proactive and develops set expectations in followers.	Reacts to situations as they are presented to them.
Uses charisma and enthusiasm as a motivator.	Uses basic reward system by providing a reward for a set goal as a motivator or punishes based on written rules or policies.
Motivates individuals by encouraging them to put the group first before their own individual interests.	Separates individuals and motivates them based on their own self-interests.
Always focusing on new ideas to improve organizational structure.	Does not deviate from the organization's structure.

Figure 1.2

Understanding the type of leader you are will allow you to better understand yourself and your role as a leader. Some departments have different needs from leadership. One that is adequately staffed with high satisfaction may support a transactional leader. A department who is overworked and have been producing record numbers may best favor from a transitional leader who will find opportunities to improve satisfaction for these individuals. As a leader, it is important to make managers understand from an employee's point of view and translate these issues and opportunities from an employee's view into a managers' perspective.

Finding unique opportunities that may be risky and untraditional is the beauty of being a leader in a non-managerial role. Being a leader gives you the freedom to take chances and make mistakes. As a leader, you should take chances that some may be afraid to, with approval of your immediate supervisor of course. Taking riskier chances as a leader is how you grow and is a prime opportunity while not in a management position. When you are in a managerial position where consequences for bigger risks are more severe, it could cost you your job, reputation, or cost the company lots of money.

Leaders may have the responsibilities that are typically performed by a manager. These responsibilities can range from scheduling, inventory management, budgeting, attending meetings, acting a liaison between other departments or companies, and oh yeah…do not forget about working your job that you were hired for as well. If others must start working harder to make up for your distractions that are brought upon by your leadership duties, then this can create discontent amongst your co-workers. Finding a good balance between your leadership duties and your daily work can be a challenge but is important to create a healthy balance between the two and keep the peace amongst your coworkers.

While we are on the topic about healthy balance, it is important to understand the importance of having a healthy work-life balance. As a leader, you must understand that although work is important, people do have personal lives that are even more important. Instead of being vengeful for a coworker calling out, understand they may have a sick child, a car that broke down and needs thousands of dollars in repairs, or may be in the middle of a divorce. Although work comprises of 25% of someone's life you need to be understanding that 75% of their life is not work and to be understanding and compassionate of this. Support those individuals by working around or with them, if possible.

As you can see, leaders have a lot on their plate. Because they tend to bite more than they can chew, leaders are often prone to experience burnout. This results in low-energy levels, losing perspective of your mission and goals, and can result in resentment towards your workplace and co-workers. Sometimes burnout can be difficult to notice. Dr. Ilfeld, an executive leadership coach, suggests looking out for these three signs of burnout:

1. You have difficulty waking up to go to work or you forget often what day of the week it is due to the lack of excitement in your job.

2. You have been mentally and physically exhausted to the point of having no interest in doing anything that you used to love, even on your days off.

3. Your moods and tempter have been out of character. You tend to present a negative attitude towards your work and portray these feelings towards your coworkers.

There are many resources that you can turn to if you start experiencing any of these feelings. Speak to your manager, HR representative, or even a career coach. They may be able to help you handle your stress and burnout as they are usually trained in handling these stressors. They may be able to assist you in having a more manageable workload and may even start to understand how much you have been taking on, which may have been overlooked. You should not look at burnout as having a negative connotation and admitting that you are in fact burnt out as a bad thing, especially if you once enjoyed your job and company. Your coworkers rather have you admit that you are burnt out and handle it rather than you bring a negative presence to work. You need to help yourself before you can help others. Finding that resource and time to sit back and relax is important to maintain a healthy drive towards your continuous leadership role.

Leaders will make recommendations through observation while managers are there to enforce these recommendations. These recommendations and ideas that are relayed to the manager are typically entertained if the leader can back it up with some data, rationalize it, and having a sense of inspiration behind the idea. Leaders not only inspire others, but also have inspiring ideas that can be beneficial for their workplace and morale. These inspiring behaviors will be discussed further in the next chapter.

"A title does not make you a leader. It is your impact and influence."

– Brigette Hyacinth, Keynote Speaker on Leadership and Human Resources

Chapter Two: Inspiring and Motivating Others

Leaders are naturally inspiring people. Leaders get their name "leader" because they lead teams. The best way great leaders lead a team is to inspire them. People that can be led by a leader are those that trust the leader to have good decision-making skills. Inspiring others occurs when you stimulate one's interest to perform equally or better than they would have without inspiration.

Inspiration typically comes from leaders, rather than managers, because they are the ones who go above and beyond their required duties. When a leader can create a positive and meaningful atmosphere for individuals, it tends to rub off on others. This, therefore, leads to inspiration for others to do the same. When you have a group of inspiring and engaged team members, the possibilities are endless.

It is important. as a leader, to understand the difference between motivation and inspiration. Motivation derives from external factors such as money, success, or a certain outcome. Inspiration means "in spirit", which comes within. When someone is inspired, they are moved by their feelings and not necessary the outcome. This chapter will discuss leadership and the importance of inspiration versus motivation. Both are important leadership traits, similar concepts, but unique in their own way. When there is no incentive for hard workers and no punishment for underperformers, motivation becomes nonexistent.

Not only do great leaders have inspiring behaviors, but also inspiring ideas. They are often creative in nature and produce such great ideas that they are enthusiastic and present it in ways that others are inspired by it as well. This may sound more like a good salesman, but because leaders focus on their coworkers needs when creating these ideas, they have the team's interest at heart. Leaders provide the support and trust for others to be inspired when normally they would not necessarily agree if it were someone else presenting the idea. Inspiration is a very motivating trait. Great leaders can create a charged atmosphere that promotes an engaging environment that people love to come to work in.

When there is lack of leadership, people tend to be disengaged and show up to work for the mere means of a paycheck at the end of the week. Do you dread going into work? If so, you most likely are either in the wrong profession or lack an inspiring leader. Even if you hate your profession, an inspiring leader can make work worthwhile and change your perception and outlook on your career. This is how powerful inspiring leaders can be on morale.

Inspiration can come in many forms and below is some of the most common reasons one may be inspired from a leader:

- Impeccable Communication

- Punctuality

- Reliability

- Gratitude

- Positivity

Without the five inspirational traits, leaders lose credibility and have a harder time in leading projects and people. Communication is my biggest pet peeve and will cover it more in depth in Chapter 6, because it is and will always be the biggest factor in any situation. Impeccable communication can go a long way as a leader because it creates a message for individuals to be aware of what is going on. Employees often deal with lack of communication within their job. Changes to policies, procedures, equipment, staff, etc. are only as effective as those who are aware of them. Leaders are typically one of the first to know about these changes and it is important to communicate these to ALL employees and not just the ones currently visible at the time.

Healthcare is especially guilty of breakdowns in communication because of the various shifts these workers have. Reaching out to these employees can be done in email form, made part of yearly evaluations, or having all employees sign and acknowledge memos. Each situation is unique, and you should assess which method is best for the information you are trying to get across.

Punctuality is another important trait that leaders must possess to be able to inspire others. Punctuality is being able to accomplish a task or goal in a designated timeframe. This includes, but not limited to, completing projects by a specific deadline, arriving to work on time, arriving early to staff meetings, and sending out reminders in an appropriate timeframe instead of a minute beforehand. As a leader, you are often looked up on by your peers. From their perspective, if you are arriving late to work without any repercussions, they will feel they have no reason to be on time either. This leads to all sorts of negative perceptions and performance in the department if others notice the lack of punctuality by leadership. Of course, there are circumstances such as being on the phone with an important client or stuck behind a bad accident. What is important is that this does not become a continued habit.

Punctuality not only shows respect and consideration but shows dependability that you can be relied upon to get things done in a timely fashion. We all know that one friend that no matter how early to make plans, they will arrive late or stall, what seems intentionally, until you are late yourself. Do not be this person, especially in a professional workplace.

The leader in your workplace may take care of the payroll for the department. Would you trust this person ever again if they forgot to submit your entire department's hours for the past payroll, which delayed your much-needed paycheck by a week? Mistakes happen but when they are important ones, that you expect a leader to carry out, it ruins the leader's reliability. We often take reliability for granted such as reliable internet, GPS to get you to your destination, a car to drive without issues, and so on. When these things are not reliable it creates a huge burden and puts a strain on the efficiency in your life. You can go from a great day to a horrible day due to lack of reliability. The same is true in the workplace. Your followers should view you as reliable because they value you, your consistency with getting the job done, and the odds that you will provide them with the correct guidance to work efficiently.

Gratitude makes better leaders because it shows that you are helpful, generous, and compassionate for their work and presence. Leaders that have higher gratitude are usually more forgiving when mistakes are made because they are understanding that no one is perfect, and mistakes are expected to be part of the process. Although a mistake may be made, they will appreciate the effort that went into the project.

Gratitude, overall, is a very important trait that brings togetherness and builds trust. However, being authentic in your gratitude is more important than the idea itself. Imagine an employee covers a last-minute callout. Although they may not say anything, they expect you, as a leader, to be happy and grateful for their commitment but instead you just say, "thanks for doing that". Being authentically grateful you would use phrases like, "thank you so much for covering their shift, this really shows your hard work and dedication for this place" or "I appreciate not only you, but also your time you are giving us and I know it is tough working extra this week but this deed will not go forgotten". Add extra flair to your gratitude and make it authentic to make it count. There is nothing worse than fake gratitude that can be spotted from a mile away.

The last trait on the list, inspiration leaders should possess, is positivity. All it takes is one negative experience to ruin a few positive. A leader who is always doing good deeds and creating a positive atmosphere can ruin how others view them with only one negative experience. For this very reason, it is important to have consistency with your positive behavior. People are so quick to judge how someone did something wrong than to compliment how someone did something well. Great leaders are ones who use their energy towards compliments rather than judging someone's mistakes or flaws. Leaders who present with positivity in the workplace tend to have teams that are in a more positive mood, have an increased job satisfaction, exhibit more engagement, and have improved performance.

They say smiles are contagious, so are positive attitudes. Those with positive and upbeat attitudes typically express enthusiasm, which others view as motivational. Toxic work cultures come from individuals who are unhappy and have negativity to express to others, which others feed on and spreads like wildfire. Be a better leader and contain that wildfire and spread positivity within your workplace, it will make the world of difference.

When you are in a work environment that does not allow you to flourish and grow, you must leave. Start somewhere else that will give you a chance and allow you to develop yourself. This may require starting off in an entry-level job and working your way into the system. If you are hardworking, engaged, and willing to learn you will have no problems climbing the ladder. A few companies that are known to promote and grow staff members that I know personally or have researched are:

- ADP

- Aldis

- American Express

- Bain & Company

- Blue Cross Blue Shield

- Charles Schwab

- Cheesecake Factory

- Enterprise Rent-A-Car

- State Farm

- Waste Management

According to an article, written by Eric Garton for Harvard Business Review, there are many attributes that make a great leader. Those who are often inspiring tend to be incredibly diverse and possess many great traits that are typically unique to the individual. The beauty of leadership is that anyone that focuses on their strengths can be inspiring to others if they hone on their skillsets to better the department and coworkers. However, those who exhibit 'centeredness' have double the chances of being seen as an inspirational leader.

What is centeredness, you ask? Centeredness is how people choose to respond to situations rather than impulsively react to it. Having this trait is important to inspire others. For example, every year your coworkers, including yourself, expect an end-of-year bonus. However, due to recent budget cuts, the bonuses are part of the cuts. As most employees will be very upset about not receiving a bonus this year, you possessing centeredness remain calm and provide reassurance to others that although the situation is not ideal at least no one's job was taken from them. Creating a negative situation into a positive outlook is important for inspiring others.

Depending on the situation, it may be very difficult to remain calm and collective. Using the three S's is important to achieve centeredness. These three S's are: Settle, Sense, and Shift. Settling yourself when you are presented in a situation you may not necessarily agree with is important and the first step to not overreact. Sensing your natural reaction to this would be the next step and requires you to notice how you feel about the situation and how you want to react. This step is important to understand how others may or will react to the situation once they find out. Lastly, shifting your emotions from negative to a more neutral or positive will allow you to make a more rational response. Going through these three steps will allow you to better handle stressful situations and process negative scenarios in a more constructive way rather than reactive. This also allows you to exhibit your inspiring leadership abilities and understand other's frustrations and turn them into neutral or positive emotions.

All it takes is one inspiring leader to set the tempo for the rest of the team. If one leader can inspire a group of co-workers, they will in return be inspiring to others. This turns into a trickle-down-effect of inspiration and creates a positive engaged workplace. Breakthroughs tend to happen when there is inspiration in the workplace because people tend to be more productive because others start setting the bar higher due to the inspiration.

As an inspiring leader, it is important to allow others to understand your mutual feelings toward an issue in the workplace. You should convey your mutual feelings and create a plan to fix or improve on the given issue. However, this should be done only if you are able to create a realistic plan of action and will follow through, or else you will lose credibility. Inspiration is a trait that comes solely from good leaders and is a trait that you will never see from a "boss". A boss provides no inspiration, but instead instills fear, which we will discuss more about how to avoid being a boss in the next chapter.

"Good leaders lead. Great leaders inspire."

-Zachary Frace, Author of *Management from the Outside*

MANAGEMENT FROM THE OUTSIDE

Chapter Three: Avoid Being a Boss

We often use the term "boss" when referring to a supervisor or manager. However, the term "boss" creates a negative connotation when referring to an immediate supervisor. A boss can be anyone that demands work to be done, create a negative presence, and is self-centered. A boss tends to take advantage of their position within an organization. Unfortunately, this occurs more often than it should and will drive the best employees away.

A leader SHOULD NEVER become a boss and a boss WILL NEVER be a leader. Bosses can be in the position of wannabe-leaders, managers, or directors. Their behavior should not exemplify what these positions are supposed to represent. These positions are intended for an elite workforce whose intentions are for the better good of the organization, patients, customers, and most importantly the employees.

These bosses are destructive for not only the department or business, but also an organization. It takes one bad apple to spoil the bunch and when it comes to management, this could not be truer. These people will usually work their way into a system or emphasize on their years of experience or education. They know who to please to justify their position regardless of many complaints they may have against them. Backhanded compliments, essentially insulting and passive-aggressive compliments, are frequently how these individuals "praise" team members. An example of this would be a boss saying, "It is amazing what great work you can do when you finally pay attention and use your brain for once.". Although these types of people are not beneficial for a successful department, they do teach leaders the importance of what not to do and how to avoid being classified as a "boss".

True leaders will be able to spot bosses from a mile away and as the old adage says, "keep your friends close and your enemies closer".... in this case, keep your co-workers and supervisors close and bosses closer. This will avoid being caught off guard and allow you to lead others more effectively if you are aware of the boss's next move.

You may be thinking, "Isn't there anything I can do?" or "Why can't the organization just get rid of them if they are such an issue?". Unfortunately, this is much easier said than done. Due to many laws, policies and the manipulative nature bosses tend to have, it is very difficult to fire someone without hard evidence of such actions. These kinds of people are confrontational in person and typically avoid texts and emails solely for this reason to avoid others being able to have physical evidence against them.

Bosses will micromanage your every move to a point where you feel uncomfortable performing your work and afraid to make a mistake, which you are now more prone to do with someone breathing down your neck. They can bring on sense of superiority, which makes employees feel inferior and worthless. These types of "managers" or "leaders" are toxic to a workplace and cause extreme discomfort amongst staff members.

When a boss is in charge, the pressure they put onto staff are often interpreted as a threat by the employee if they do not perform to expectations because they feel they may be fired or talked to in a demeaning way. Great leaders turn these pressures into challenges for the staff to accomplish. For example, if a boss is demanding an idea to increase sales by 5% by the end of the day or performance appraisals will be affected a good leader will turn this situation into a challenge. The challenge could be in a form of a game or contest that will include a group collaboration and whoever choses the best idea wins. Prizes can range from monetary incentives, gift cards, parties, or even a personal day off. Turning a negative situation into a fun and uplifting one is just one of the many characteristic's great leaders possess.

An even bigger issue is when your co-worker, someone not in a supervisory position, starts acting like your manager in a bossy way. This happens very frequently in workplaces that lack proper management or leadership. When employees feel that management is not doing enough or is never present that they must step up into a leadership role themselves, however they lack the fundamentals that it takes to be a great leader.

This individual stepping into a leadership role without fundamentals or knowledge may mean well, however when there is lack of management to control the situations, it can get out of hand. An example of this would be when a manager leaves an organization and there is now a vacant managerial position. This position is not in a rush to get filled by senior management and, therefore, an employee or two may feel the need to step up and take control of certain day-to-day operations. This is great that there are employees willing to step up, however one of the employees started to make lists of duties for everyone to get done each week. Each list of duties is sloppily put together and has no rhyme or reason and simply consist of things that must be done. Being told to do something by anyone other than a supervisor or manager can come off as bossy and can lead to a lot of trouble within a department. Employee A tells this bossy employee that they are unable to complete the tasks because they feel uncomfortable completing something that they are not trained for. The bossy employee then goes and tells them that they need to complete it or there will be issues in the department and it will put everyone else behind.

Telling your co-workers that they must complete something "or else" is not something that should ever be done as a leader in a non-supervisory position. The issue with this scenario is that although the bossy employee meant well to make sure duties would be completed, they did not methodically plan the duties per other's strengths. It should have been carried out as a team project and offer any help as needed. The lack of managerial presence sets up opportunities for employees to overstep their boundaries with their co-workers and can cause much discord.

If you are in a position where you are not the supervisor or manager but need tasks completed by your peers, you should approach them with a team mindset. Ask them if they mind completing a project because you think they would be the best person to get it accomplished in a timely manner and offer the support and availability to help them if they need it. This creates a much smoother and positive workplace when you work with your peers and not against them by being the "boss" and demanding work to be done when it is not your place to do so. To best accomplish this, it is best to understand those you work with on a personal level. I am not talking about knowing their middle name or their darkest secret, but rather their personality traits based on professional assessments.

Professional personality assessments are used in some organizations for managers to better understand their direct reports. However, it is important for co-workers to understand each other's personality assessments to be able to work better in teams. Not every workplace has managers that directly oversee every aspect of the department and often allow co-workers to independently work together without direct supervision. As a leader, recommend to management that it would be beneficial for your entire team to take one of the many assessments to create better collaboration and understanding of co-worker's strengths and weaknesses, which will directly help with teamwork.

There are many assessments you can recommend such as the Myers-Briggs Type Indicator, DISC Assessment, The Hogan Personality Inventory (HPI), and The SHL Occupational Personality Questionnaire. Some psychologists argue that some tests are better than the other, but it primarily depends on what you are trying to get out of the assessments. Are you looking to use it for recruitment purposes? Then the HPI would be the best assessment. Or are you trying to understand your co-workers better? Then the MBTI would be a better option. A breakdown of these four assessments will be discussed in more detail on Figure 3.1.

Type	Utilization	Description	Price
MBTI	Most popular 93-question assessment that requires matching a word with a statement. Separates individuals by Extrovert vs. Introvert, Intuition vs. Sensing, Thinking vs. Feeling, and Judging vs. Perceiving. Users will be categorized out of 16 possible combinations and classifies them as their matched personality such as "ESTJ".	Individual/employee development, increase productivity, and improve efficiencies. Used for better communication and delegation geared towards others personality types. Could also be used for recruitment purposes.	Personal Price $49.95 Business Plan - includes "team portal" and tips for team building. $89.95/pp
DISC	DISC assessments can range from a short to long assessment but typically consist of 78-80 questions that	Increase self-knowledge to know what motivates you and stressors. Improve working relationships by understanding others behavioral	Many tests from different vendors. Typically range from $64.50-

	measures individual's primary traits between Dominate, Influential, Steady, and Compliant. Evaluates behavioral differences.	style. Teaches productive conflict.	79/pp.
HPI	HPI is a 15-20 minute 206 true/false question assessment that evaluates service orientation, stress tolerance, reliability, clerical potential, sales potential, and managerial potential.	Predicts job performance and satisfaction. Use to assess whether leaders and managers will fit the organizational culture.	Can range from $30-400 depending on the services needed.
SHL	Can be referred to as "OPQ32" that consist of 104 questions that measures 32 different characteristics. Uses three domains:	Questions are tailored specifically for within the workplace unlike other assessments that focus on general personality traits both in and out of the workplace.	Price varies depending on pricing model. Typical costs are roughly $250 for the one-

	Relationships with people, thinking style and feelings, and emotions. User is presented with 4 statements and must pick the one that is least relevant to them. Assesses your style and preferences and how they align with your role at work.	Use to eliminate candidates during recruitment process, identify future leaders, and identify strengths for development purposes.	time assessment.

Figure 3.1 Assessment Types

Typically, a manager would be encouraging these assessments to be completed by their employees. As a leader it is important to present these assessments to the manager if they are not already part of your workplace. The pushback will be that they can be expensive for an organization that has many employees. The benefit of these assessments can far outweigh the cost if they are utilized correctly.

A leader pushes collaboration and teamwork and these assessments have been used by many companies to improve teams and recruit the best candidates to fit the open position. In fact, 89 of the Fortune 100 companies use the MTBI before hiring an employee. If and when you are able to convince management to purchase these assessments, encourage participation and open-sharing of results so that you are to better understand individual's personality type so you can improve communication and understanding of their preferences. Some results of yourself and co-workers may be obvious, however you may be surprised by the results.

As a leader that may have a "boss" as a manager/supervisor, you should encourage them to participate and share results of these assessments with the team. When employees can see the results of their boss, they are able to learn their personality type and be able to understand what makes them "tick" to avoid any issues. Bosses may even be surprised by their own results, therefore allowing self-reflection and possible changes to their demeanor. These assessments are a great tool for all and can be classified as a learning tool, which we will discuss more about learning in the next chapter.

"The key to successful leadership today is influence, not authority. "

- Kenneth Blanchard, Author of multiple leadership books

MANAGEMENT FROM THE OUTSIDE

Chapter Four: Never Stop Learning

If you are reading this book, it is for a reason. You are looking to learn more and grow yourself professionally, which is exactly what this chapter is about. Learning can come in many forms and is not limited solely to formal education. Learning can come in the form of, but not limited to, the following: formal education, continuing education credits, reading relevant print/online journals, networking with people of similar professional backgrounds, obtaining certifications, YouTube videos, and even non-credited courses related to your profession and personal interest at local colleges offered in the afternoon and/or weekends to suite working individuals.

Formal education is the most obvious form of education and can also be one of the most expensive investments one can make. Notice how I used the word "investment" because that is exactly what education is. Formal education can be any type of higher education after high school and can also include trade schools and certificate programs. The most common pathway is for high school students to decide between going to college or a trade school to achieve their career goals. However, deciding on what type of educational institution to pursue and what major to go for is a very difficult decision as a senior in high school let alone adults in their 20's and 30's. According to the United States Department of Education, 33% of students change their major at least once and 10% change it more than once. This is due to the extreme pressure of choosing the "right" path at such an early stage of adulthood. One way that this can be fixed is by shadowing a list of careers that interests you most, if able, to provide an effective way to allow students to make a better educated decision by experiencing it firsthand.

Trade school should not be overlooked because it is a field that is struggling to get candidates due to society and high schools emphasizing to juniors and seniors that they must go to college to succeed. This is obviously not true as trade schools are a fraction of the cost of colleges and have a high demand for new graduates. However, professionally speaking, it is very difficult to grow up the ladder within an organization without a college degree. This is not to say that those who attend trade schools cannot successfully run their own businesses, but this is for those looking to grow professionally in an already established organization.

Companies are making it harder and harder to enter the professional realm without many years of experience and education from an accredited college. Most job postings that are supervisory in nature require a minimum of a bachelor's degree in business management, or a related degree, and typically prefer a master's degree in business administration with many years of experience. The higher the position, the higher education should be typically expected. It is possible that a CEO may have no formal education, but with the push on educational requirements most will require new entrants to have an MBA or doctorate degree with a minimum of 10+ years of experience.

Education is very important when it comes to management positions, but not as important as the employee's experiences, character, and attributes. Human Resources understands just because one has a required degree does not, however, make them qualified for a position. An employee's career encapsulates many forms of attributes such as involvement in past projects, years in the field, success, their personality, experiences, contacts, and of course, education.

Becoming a successful manager or improving on your management skills requires much more than experience and past education. Continuous learning is vital to be able to provide your employees with all the necessary tools to perform their job successfully. Regardless of your current position or level of education, there is always a next step for you. A CEO of a hospital that started as a nurse that who just earned their PhD in business years later is still capable of continuous learning opportunities. They can get their degree in finance so they can better understand and make sound financial decisions alongside the CFO or maybe they take an online marketing course to help the struggling marketing team. There should never be an excuse to not continue learning.

Continuing education or professional development is required for many professionals in many different fields. The purpose of continuing education is to stay current with the latest trends, skills, technologies, and more. These are sometimes mandatory for professionals to remain certified with certifications in which may require continuing education units, or commonly known as CEUs. The purpose of these are to keep professionals relevant in their certifications and field. Although these credits are often performed in the quickest and cheapest method it is important to understand the opportunities that these credits and development courses can have on your career.

Instead of being someone who is just taking these credits to solely "get them over with" be the person who makes the most of these learning opportunities. Pick topics that are something you are interested in but do not have much knowledge in. If you are an emergency room nurse and you have an opportunity to perform your CEUs about NICU nursing that you have little knowledge on and interests you, take that course! You may be presented with an opportunity to manage a NICU and having general knowledge because of your CEUs will give you that advantage you otherwise would not have had. Do not miss opportunities because you are looking for an easy way out or do not think you have time to learn something new. Most CEUs are due every year or every other, which equates to 8,760 hours each year. Excuses that there is not enough time to learn new material, especially if it interest you, is not a true excuse. To get ahead in your professional career, you must be willing to learn and develop yourself every opportunity you can, and these are the perfect opportunities to develop your knowledge.

The past twenty years have changed our learning to have endless possibilities. There are many different platforms from which you can learn from. For example, I obtained my bachelor's degree in Medical Imaging right after high school in four years, which is common. My first job was as an X-ray and CT Scan technologist, which I was required to obtain my CT scan certification within a year. I self-taught myself, through books and online courses, and took my boards within that timeframe. The day after I completed that, I looked at what the next step is for me. It took me a year and a half to decide if I wanted to get my MRI certification, go back to school for business since I've always had interest in my own business, and many other options that I could not decide on. After further research, obtaining my MBA with a concentration in Healthcare Administration was most likely my best course of action and was able to do it all online while being able to work fulltime. I then got certificates online for project management and Six Sigma Green Belt. As you can see, there are many ways you can learn and should have no excuses to not find new continuing education opportunities.

Whether I decide to stick to the healthcare field or own my own business, this degree will be beneficial for whatever career I decide to choose. Sticking to a minor or concentration to your "backup" or other interest in life can be very beneficial down the road if you ever decide to change career paths. Therefore, I chose this specific degree because it tailored to my specific needs and interests.

Online degrees have become a very popular option as it gives students the freedom to complete coursework around their work schedules and therefore can be completed by any professional that is unable to take a year or two off of work. Online education has had a bad reputation when it was first developed, but with new software, requirements, and accreditations, it is just as respectable as "traditional" education.

Advice:

Make sure whatever degree you lean towards, make sure that it is of interest to you and will be thirty years down the line. The school should be accredited because there are some programs out there that promise XYZ degree but are not nationally recognized, which is very important to consider. Whatever you decide to do, remember that you are ultimately your own coach in life. Your decisions will ultimately affect the outcome of your life. Sitting back and relaxing and you will lose most of the time. Hard work and practice will produce winning outcomes. As my coach always said, "be happy with your success, but never be satisfied".

Being a great leader or manager is not always about the certificate, title, or degree you have. I have on countless times seen doctors asking nurses medical questions and managers asking employees questions that pertain to management. Great workplaces are structured where you have multiple layers of education, experiences, and skillsets that creates dynamics. It allows someone to have a weakness or lack a skillset because you will have someone else that does possess that skillset. An example of this would be a small consulting company. Consultant A is great at utilizing datasets and analytics but lacks general accounting principles. Consultant B is a CPA who is horrible at analytics and noticing trends. Combine these two together and they will compensate each other's weaknesses and be a dynamic duo.

Some professions, particularly in the medical field, require health professionals to complete continuing education credits. Although some look at these credits only as necessary requirements to keep their license, they should be viewed as opportunities. Many credits can be chosen by the user and should be selected 50% on your interest and 50% on topics that are unknown to you. This way you have a spread of interesting topics mixed with topics that are foreign and require you to learn more about, which makes you more knowledgeable than the day before, which is what this entire chapter is about. Now that we emphasized the importance of education, we will now focus on building relationships, which is just another important part of being a great leader.

"Once you stop learning, you start dying."

-Albert Einstein, Well-known theoretical physicist

MANAGEMENT FROM THE OUTSIDE

Chapter Five: Building Relationships

Relationships come in many forms, ranging from personal to professional. There are four primary relationship group. The groups include family relationships, acquaintances, friendships, and romantic relationships. It may seem that for relevant purposes we would only be discussing acquaintances however, to be a good leader it is important to understand and build upon all four of the relationship groups you have.

Family relationships are strong bonds that typically last a lifetime. In a traditional setting, parents are the first ones to guide future leaders. Parents who raise good leaders often allowed the child to solve problems for themselves, encourage creativity, improve their communication skills, and supported their decisions throughout all stages of life. Although there is not much you can do about how you were raised, good leaders often come from those with strong family relationships.

Acquaintances are not friends nor family. They are ones you have frequent contact with but do not know on a personal level. They can be neighbors, co-workers, and members of your church. As a leader, co-workers do not have to cross into your personal realm. However, it is important to still understand their differences, likes/dislikes, and challenges they may be facing at work. They may open up that they need a little extra time to complete a project because they are having some issues at home or they have some medical problems they may have been dealing with. As a leader this is all you need to know and to also be empathetic of. However, if this coworker

45

told you the specific family or medical problem they were having and you choose to discuss it more after work then this may lead to a friendship, which is the next type of relationship.

Friendships are important for leaders because to advance within your career it is important to know the right connections and people that will give you a chance. Mentors, for example, may start out as acquaintances and someone you looked up to, such as a manager. As you develop yourself professionally this manager may someday become your mentor and help guide you through the course of your career. Manager-employee friendships should be avoided if there is direct supervision to avoid favoritism. Once there is no direct supervision, this mentor may become your friend and will be an asset to your career. Overall, friendships are important because friends are to be supportive and will often tell you the truth, even when it hurts. This differs from a family or romantic relationship, where they may be less willing to tell you the truth and may even embellish the facts to be less harsh. This is important when trying to receive honest and constructive feedback.

Romantic relationships are not always necessary but make your support system even stronger. This type of relationship provides one with a sense of belonging when you can come home to someone every day after work and tell your entire day to. This person is one you can trust and typically share very similar interests that allow you to bounce ideas that may support you on your leadership journey. Like friends, this person is there to support you on your journey. Romantic relationships can either be extremely supportive or can sometimes hinder your growth depending on how compatible the both of you are. If you are a risk taker and your romantic relationship plays it safe, they may prevent you from going back to school.

Although mentors were discussed more so in the friendship portion, they can derive from any of the four types of relationships. It can be your parent, friend, acquaintance, or your significant other. There is not much literature on the topic but there are essentially three types of mentorships that one can have, which are personal, professional, and indirect. All three of these mentorships are important in their own way. One should have a healthy balance between all three to make the most out of being a mentored.

A personal mentorship can come from anyone that you have a close bond with, such as a best friend, family member, or family friend. These personal mentors can usually provide guidance in a personalized approach in ways that profession and indirect mentors cannot. Personal mentors will be able to help you achieve more of your personal goals and may give you more of a solid foundation on developing your soft skills. They play a strong presence in your personal life that is fundamental for how you act because your bond is stronger towards these individuals while growing up. If your mentor is your father and he was a hard worker, polite, and fearless you most likely will exhibit the same traits as him. Although you may act differently in your personal life versus professional, you will still carry around your personal behaviors into your professional life. Therefore, it is important to make sure you have positive personal mentors in your life, because they know your true self, which is the foundation in which you base all your decisions.

A professional mentor, on the other hand, may not know you on a personal level, such as a manager, teacher, or coach. Your professional mentors will most likely know your strengths, weaknesses, goals, and personality where they are able to guide you in a more constructed way that they believe would work best for you. These mentors can provide important guidance but in a less personalized approach and can be equally as effective. These professional mentors may know you more on a professional level and are able to help you achieve your professional goals. A football coach, for example, does not need to know your personal obstacles to be a good coach and mentor. If you are uncertain with your sexual preference, the coach does not need to know this to help guide you to be a better football player and person. These mentors will be able to help you more with your hard skills and developing yourself into bigger professional roles. They are great to use for references and may also be more able to help you be a mentor for others as well.

An indirect mentor is just how it sounds. It is a mentor who indirectly influences you based on their demeanor, influential posts, and success. An example of this would be following Mark Cuban, an influential entrepreneur, owner of the Dallas Mavericks, and investor on ABC's *Shark Tank* on social media platforms. Mark Cuban often posts influential material on his LinkedIn and can be a good indirect mentor for business-minded people looking for a motivational push. "Influencers" are a very popular and modern trend, but do not need to be limited to just those who post random YouTube videos looking for their 5-minutes of fame. There are many real influencers out there that are in very successful roles and positions and actively engage with members. They can range from motivational speakers, CEOs, authors, athletes, and so on. These individuals will most likely never know who you are, but their success and overcoming their failures can be the encouragement you need to lead you towards taking chances you otherwise might not have.

Now that you know the different kinds of mentors there are…what makes a mentor a good mentor? You may read or think that a good mentor is a good influence, someone who is successful, has a positive attitude, and is a great leader. Although these are excellent attributes of a good mentor, a great mentor is someone that will help you in your pursuit of success through whatever means possible geared towards your personal or professional needs. For example, if you have great leadership skills but you lack confidence, you may benefit from a mentor who exhibits all the traditional mentor-like qualities but excels in confidence. If none of your current mentors have a lot of confidence, find an indirect mentor who strives on confidence and listen to a podcast or webinar that they may have been featured in. Follow them on social media platforms and learn from them. Understand your flaws, embrace them, and find someone that will be able to help you transform your weaknesses.

Aside from mentorship, there are many opportunities in this digital world that you can develop relationships and market yourself in endless capacities. There are many routes you can choose to meet new people and network. Many cities offer groups and clubs, and some are even national organizations that will allow you to connect more with others and can be included on your resume. Below is a list of good organizations to join if you are looking to build better relationships.

- Rotary Club- international service organization that brings together business and professional leaders to provide humanitarian service, and to advance goodwill and peace around the world. It is a non-political and non-religious organization open to anyone looking to join. Starts at $260/year for a membership.

- Lions Club International- international non-political organization that promotes principles of good government and citizenship. It is an excellent club to develop leadership skills and give back to the community. Starts at $35 as an entrance fee.

- Chamber of Commerce- organization that supports local businesses and allows volunteers to network with business owners and other members with similar interests. Businesses can also join the commerce to better network and promote their business. Business memberships are around $200-400 and volunteering for the commerce is typically free.

- United Way Young Leaders Society- international network of young professionals from their early-20s to mid-40s who share a passion for advancing community solutions locally and globally. Many opportunities are provided such as mentoring young individuals, having lunch with business owners, and any other opportunities that allow you to use your expertise to make a difference. Great for networking and enhancing your skillset. Free and has a list of volunteer opportunities that is categorized by an array of interest.

- ToastMasters International- networking group that focuses on improving upon networking and improving your five core competencies of public speaking, interpersonal communication, strategic leadership, management, and confidence. Has a collection of clubs that fits your interests and will allow you to network with others with similar interests. Cost $65 for new members.

As you can see, there are many opportunities that allow you to connect with others. Some of these groups are more demanding than others and require introverts to come out of their shell to meet with groups of strangers. If you are looking for something with less of an interaction with others, MeetUp despite its name is another great tool that will help others build relationships with other like-minded individuals. With Covid-19, these groups are being held in an online format and allows groups of people to discuss certain issues and topics that are of interest to you. For example, I am interested in consulting. I searched consulting and pages of results populated. Some including networking, some included how-to's, and others offered tips and tricks. This website can be used for multiple reasons such as hobbyist, volunteers, professional networking, and just a platform to discuss an array of topics. Joining is free and hosting events usually cost $15/month. You can use this for whatever interest you most but make the most of it and try to network to meet new people. You never know who you may meet. Afterall, it could be your next boss, a new friend, or even a future mentor.

Although online has many opportunities to connect with others, simply getting out of the house sets yourself up for opportunities to connect with others. For example, going out to the bar for a drink after work can open a window of opportunity to meet someone new. It may even be the CEO of a top company you have had strong interest in for the past few years and set yourself into a future role with that company. Without getting out of the house, you would never have had that opportunity in the first place.

You are always told to talk less about yourself and listen more to others. This is not necessarily true when you are trying to connect with new people. Yes, you should listen to what others have to say but also let people know who you are, what your goals are, and what interest you. For example, attending your son's football game gives you the chance to talk to one of the other parents. You mention that you just obtained your MBA in Healthcare Administration and that you have been looking for a job that aligns with your recent degree. It turns out that this parent is the VP of Operations at the local hospital and has an opening that they highly encourage you to apply to. Without talking about your recent accomplishment, you may have never had this opportunity.

It is not always easy talking about yourself and your accomplishments, especially to strangers. However, to be a good communicator and build lasting relationships, you tend to have more to talk about when you find out when others share similar interests as you and can build lasting relationships not just personally but also professionally. If you are the kind of person who has difficulty in these situations, I have a challenge for you: Put yourself in a situation that is uncomfortable for yourself. Find out what makes you feel uncomfortable about meeting new people. Is it a fear of rejection, unsure if you will be compatible, or just have difficulty of thinking of what to talk about? Before you put yourself in that situation think about your fear and how to overcome it. Think of topics to talk about, be fearless, and be open to conflicting ideas or feelings. The more you put yourself out there, the more comfortable you will become and the more relationships you will start to build.

Building relationships are not only good for your professional wellbeing but also your personal. Great leaders have great relationships with almost everyone they come across. If you have a bad relationship with someone, find out why and fix it. You do not need to become best friends, but you need to be professional and have a working relationship. You never know when you may need that person in your court, and it is important to have as many people on your side when you need them the most. This wraps up our leadership portion. We will next discuss the different components of how to become a better manager.

"Business is all about relationships...how well you build them determines how well they build your business..."

-Brad Sugars, Business and Wealth Coach

MANAGEMENT FROM THE OUTSIDE

Part II: Becoming A Better Manager

Part II will focus on becoming a better manager. As discussed before, managers can be leaders, but this chapter will focus on managers who are already in a management role and how they can improve in said role. Managers, compared to leaders, are held to a higher standard and accountability.

Leaders who excel and provide results will eventually land themselves into an official management position. Once given this title as manager, it is important to uphold your standards and all your skills and qualities that landed you into the position in which you are in now. From an employee's standpoint, a good manager is not one that will know everything, it will be the one that they are able to rely on and know they will fight tooth and nail for their employees and department. Being a reliable manager is only one of the many traits you must possess. Being a manager also requires soft skills, and the leadership skills discussed in the first half of the book, to be successful. Once you have perfected your leadership skills and qualities, it is now time to work on becoming a better manager.

There are many great managers that are full of knowledge, experience, and skillsets but lack common leadership skills. Being a manager is more than having great ideas and visions. It requires driving a group of people towards success. Some companies will hire the most experienced and oldest team member to fulfill a management position without giving them the proper resources to set them up for success. This is the equivalent of a remote without batteries. It has potential to work, but without the proper resources, it'll never work.

In the following chapters we will discuss the hiring process. This is where you will be faced with the decision on whether to hire internally or externally. This section will also be focused on improving communication as a manager that will include not only verbal communication but also how listening is equally as important in the communication process. We will discuss the many responsibilities that managers have in their roles. The following chapter will be unique as it will view an idea that I coined called, "personal quality assurance". This is a modified form of quality assurance that holds the manager responsible for improving themself. The book will then wrap up on the last chapter that will focus on two topics, which is the proper and improper use of social media and will also tie in the importance of appreciation for your team.

"Bad managers tell employees what to do, good managers explain why they need to do it, but great managers involve people in the decision making and improvement."

– Mark Graban, Lean Consultant

Chapter Six: Internal vs. External Hire

Being a manager can be daunting overseeing multiple people, all with different needs. You are supposed to be a role model for your department, have all the right answers when asked questions, ensure budgets are maintained, develop employee and customer satisfaction, attend meetings, and everything in between. On top of all these duties, one of the most important parts of being a manger is being involved and invested in the hiring process. Success recruitment practices sets the foundation for competent and successful team members.

Managers are like scouts for the NFL; they need to build the best team possible from external sources to deliver the best team. The best of players or employees may cost more due to their talents and if they cannot be afforded, then essential resources must be utilized to strengthen the current team you have at hand, which is also the responsibility of the manager, or coach. The question for managers to consider when hiring is if they search externally for the best possible candidate or if they should promote from within by developing their team/individuals who are motivated to move vertically within an organization. This is a dilemma that managers must face and choose the best course of action is best for their department. Positions must be thought about not only for current needs but for future needs as well. Never hire to just fill a spot that is empty. Having a plan and executing it should be thought out and not spontaneous.

A supervisory position opens in the department or organization and you have the responsibility of hiring the perfect candidate. Hiring internally typically makes the most strategic sense for many reasons. As a manager you should have a good idea of what approach you will be making to fill a supervisory position in your department. Before you do, make sure you have all the options laid out on the table because rushing this type of decision can have a large negative impact on the department. The pros and cons listed below may be able to help ease the decision-making process and put you in the right direction for your next hire.

Pros for Hiring Internally

➢ **Less Risk**- Managers should already know their employee's strengths and weaknesses for the position.

➢ **Quicker Adaptation**- Employees should already be acclimated to departmental policies, equipment, staff, etc., which reduces the amount of training needed.

➢ **Cheaper**- Less time spent on training and recruitment (if their position does not need to be filled).

➢ **Acclimation Period**- There can be a contingency that the hired employee will start their new role once their replacement, if applicable, is acclimated to their role. This gives them the opportunity to get prepared for their new role.

➢ **Increase Engagement**- Employees will be more engaged if there are opportunities available to them.

Depriving them of these opportunities gives them little to strive for.

Cons for Hiring Internally

➤ **Lowers Morale-** Hiring internally can negatively impact the morale of the department if someone who is not considered as strong of a candidate who ends up getting the position.

➤ **Lower Respect for Authority-** There can be a loss of respect if the person that is hired internally is not well liked or not viewed as the best candidate. This can be an issue if this person is hired for an authoritative position.

➤ **Unlikely to Change-** Internal hires are less likely to drastically change the processes of a department due to being in the same environment for a given time.

Pros Hiring Externally

➤ **Expanding Options-** This allows for a larger applicant pool, which can turn up many well-qualified applicants.

➤ **New Perspectives-** "Fresh set of eyes". External candidates offer new ideas and perspectives that can turn a "dull" department into a flourishing one.

➢ **Needed Change-** If there are internal issues that need to be changed, external candidates will have better success in carrying these out because they are not emotionally invested in the department/co-workers that may not agree with the necessary changes.

Cons Hiring Externally

➢ **Internal Unappreciation-** Internal candidates will feel unappreciated that they looked and hired externally.

➢ **Not Taken Seriously-** Internal candidates will feel they are not taken seriously.

➢ **Time-** Time to train, develop, and get an external candidate up to speed can take months versus an internal candidate.

➢ **Cost-** Time is money. The amount of extra training and cost of external recruitment can be expensive.

➢ **Unpredictable-** May be well-qualified but may not be the best fit or have the best personality needed for the position.

The breakdown above should serve as a guide to aide in the decision-making process, however each situation is unique. Externally hiring can make more sense in one situation but internally hiring can make more sense in another. When a department is failing, there is poor morale, or they are not producing an expected outcome, external recruitment should be highly considered. Having an outside source be able to get a fresh set of eyes on the workflow and to be able to search for talents or skills that the department is lacking can be a deciding factor to hire externally. An example of this would be if there has been money that went missing and unaccounted for, a manager with an accounting degree or lots of experience in finances is recommended to fill as an external position.

There is a common misconception that a position must be posted externally. This may be true based on organizational policies, federal positions that must offer veterans an equal opportunity, or any organization involved in a collective bargaining agreement. Otherwise, if you are not required to post externally only do so if you have full intentions of going through proper interviews and have a lack of potential internal candidates. Online applications can take up to an hour to complete, onsite interviews typically require the candidate to take time off their current job, uncompensated travel, and so on. When conducting interviews, you should never keep an interviewee waiting for more than 15 minutes. Not only is it disrespectful and unprofessional, it makes a horrible first impression. It shows that if the interviewees time is not valued that their time will not be valued as an employee. Also, do not waste others time if there are no true intentions of hiring externally. Pull the position as soon as it is filled. This cannot be stressed enough. Not only does it inconvenience the external candidates but also puts internal candidates on edge because they know they may have external competition and feel betrayed that they are not good enough to fill the position.

As mentioned before, hiring is a unique process and should be evaluated for the needs of the department. If the decision is to go internally, then you must think about their current position. Do you fill it with someone of equal attributes? Is there a void in a set of skills that the department may need? Or, can this position go unfilled? Hiring internally can open a gate of many opportunities for that replacement position.

Finding the perfect candidate is only a portion of the recruitment process. Considering the cost that goes along with recruitment should also be addressed. There are multiple studies out there that evaluate recruitment costs, replacement costs, and training costs. Replacing an employee can cost 150-200% of their annual salary. An indirect cost is the time spent from others training new employees with the average employer losing 3 months of productivity by training new employees. Utilizing temporary employees just increases these costs dramatically and should only be used in dire situations. Chasing external candidates, when you have well-qualified internal candidates, can be a very costly mistake if not done for the right reasons. Post the position internally for two weeks and if no one shows interest then post externally. One week is too short of a period and someone who is off during that week may miss the opportunity, which could be the one who has wanted this position the most.

Career development is one of the top five "must-haves" at work. Developing your employees that you already have should be important for satisfaction, engagement, and retainment. Promotions or internally hiring an existing employee will accomplish this career development in the workplace and will be able to free up their position with talent that is necessary for the department. For example, a radiology department may have a radiology supervisor position available. Two technologists that are certified in both X-ray and CT scan are interested in developing their professional careers and apply to the position. As the manager, you have been noticing a void in MRI where they are constantly short staffed. A smart move would be to select the best internal candidate for the supervisory position and fill the new empty position with someone who has X-ray, CT, and MRI certifications. This would not only fill the supervisory position with talent that you are familiar with but also help MRI, which could have been overlooked without looking at all aspects of how the hiring decision can affect the entire department.

When the manager decides if he/she will go externally or internally, there are steps that should be taken that are broken down below.

Internal

> Develop or fill a vacant position.

> Decide between internally or externally hiring.

> If promoting, make sure they accept it before announcing it among others.

> Internal posting should be up long enough interested individuals to apply. Formal interviews should be held.

➢ If there is a candidate who stands out before the interviews, but someone else stands out during interviews that was unexpected, hold a second round for the top 2 or 3 candidates.

➢ After your chosen candidate accepts the offer, you should announce the news with the department and what to expect in next few weeks

External

➢ Develop or fill a vacant position.

➢ Before posting the shift externally, explain to the staff why it is posted externally before they see it for themselves. Explain that internal candidates are welcome to apply as well.

➢ If there is not a rush to fill the position, do not rush to the 1st candidate with matching qualifications.

➢ Perform onsite interviews with a meet-and-greet session with staff so they can give feedback. This can be very valuable.

➢ Select the best candidate that fits the budgeted salary and department needs.

Following these steps will follow the best recruitment practices and ensuring that all employees are being carefully addressed and communicated with along the entire process. No matter the situation, some employees will be against the decision. Unfortunately, not everyone will be happy with your decisions. Being honest and open about the process is important for clarification of the decisions made. Communication, discussed in the next chapter, will cover how important it is to communicate with employees through important decision-making processes that will ultimately affect them. Not all decisions regarding hiring will be foolproof. Hiring externally is very risky for the fact that a resume and an interview can go so well because they know just what to say and can put on a big smile. However, their personality and performance can be far from what they presented in the interview. Every situation is unique, but studies suggest that internally hiring is the best choice for employee satisfaction, engagement, costs, and reduces the overall risk of hiring externally.

"If you hire the right people the first time who are willing to grow and succeed, you should have no doubt whether to hire internally for an even better position than they are in now."

- Zachary Frace, Author of *Management from the Outside*

MANAGEMENT FROM THE OUTSIDE

Chapter Seven: Communication

Communication is everything. Communication is so huge that dozens of books are written about the topic alone. I can bore you with the details from how communication developed through the early ages of civilization, however we are here to talk about the use of effective communication in the workplace. It is the framework of any type of business because it requires communication from employees talking to clients, the company talking to governing bodies, employees talking to each other, and most importantly managers talking to their employees.

So much information can be translated by simple forms of communication or missed from lack thereof. I prefer the word "effective communication" because it involves clear communication that gets the point across to the listener(s). Communication is only as effective as the one communicating it and the receiver interpreting it. Imagine working in the healthcare field where a busy doctor is telling a nurse to deliver 60 milligrams of fentanyl status-post surgery versus the recommended 55-75 micrograms/ml. These two doses to a non-clinical reader may not sound like a huge difference, however one is enough to reduce pain after surgery while the other is enough to kill a full-sized elephant. Granted, there are many safeguards in place to prevent this from happening but the point being is that effective communication is vital to successfully perform tasks with others.

As a manager, you are expected to have the answers for your employee's questions, ideas, thoughts, and everything in between. They rely on you to convey all messages and information to them that they believe is pertinent to their job. Sometimes managers may not think messages or information needs to be shared, but transparency is important for trust between managers and employees. However, be careful not to be transparent about everything. Use discretion when the information is confidential or private information about other employees.

One of my biggest pet peeves is managers who do not respond to their employee's emails in a timely manner, or even at all. As a manager, it is your duty to respond to these emails to not only entertain the thoughts of your employees but to also show that you care about their thoughts, ideas, and feelings. A delay in communication can also cause rumors to spread, especially if you hold off telling people about a sensitive topic such as potential layoffs. There is a lot of pressure on managers to be perfect and to have all the answers right away. It is okay if you do not have all the answers that will allow you to email an answer back right away. However, employees are still expecting you to send a response, such as:

"(Employees Name),

I have received your email. I appreciate the feedback/concern and I cannot give you an exact answer at this time. However, I will find the answer to your question/concern shortly or find someone that can.

Thank you for all you do,

(Manager's Name)"

Not responding to your staff can create a lot of frustration as well as a decrease in employee engagement. If employees are not taken seriously by not being responded to in a timely manner, they feel as though their opinions do not matter and will therefore not go above and beyond in the future. Having open effective communication with your employees will not only create empathy but should open a door of opportunities between managers and staff. Creating an open channel to discuss issues, ideas, opportunities, and goals creates a support network for employees to resort to. Many managers create focus groups that meet once a month, or as necessary, to allow open communication and share ideas. These groups help empower employees and allowing teamwork to solve problems particularly those that are ongoing and allow a no-fault environment. This all cannot be possible without active engagement from the manager. If a manager tends to ignore emails or not engage in effective communication, it creates a tension within the workplace and ceases the potential on an operational standpoint.

Communication can be uncomfortable for some people, especially in interviews, performance reviews, reprimanding someone, or talking about sensitive information. In the workplace, it is okay to have someone else there to witness your conversations. As a manager it is important to understand that employees may take some forms of communication and misunderstand the information you intended. Having a witness, such as an HR representative, present during reprimands or poor performance appraisals can be beneficial so information is not misconstrued.

Most employees have good intentions, whether they are right or not is a different story. However, entertaining any idea an employee may have is always recommended. If an employee has a cost-saving idea that will save the company thousands of dollars per year listen and take good notes. More importantly, take action if the idea is attainable. Allow them to be a part of and lead this project. Also, allow them to take credit for it, it was their idea after all. This allows the employee to feel a sense of contribution. Listening to employees and taking notes, but not acting or following up with those employees, can have the opposite effect. Be careful of not losing these high achievers who strive to focus on quality improvement initiatives.

Delivering your thoughts into words may sound easy, however when put into uncomfortable or stressful situations, it can be much easier said than done. No pun intended. As a manager, you must face very uncomfortable situations such as dealing with an employee's FMLA paperwork due to a death in a family, laying off a single mother, or interviewing someone who gives uncomfortable answers that makes you question their character. There are typically two types of personalities in the world.

Instead of looking at extroverts as outgoing, loud, and boisterous we should be understanding of how their inner extroversion works, which will be discussed below. Also, the same is true for introverts, instead of looking as these individuals as shy and timid individuals, understanding them in a more meaningful way is important for successful leadership. You can be an introvert or an extrovert or fall somewhere in between depending on the situation, but it is most important to be able to classify not only those you are leading but also where you fall into the spectrum to be able to develop stronger relationships.

As mentioned previously an introvert is neither better nor worse than an extrovert. People sometimes get stereotyped based on these classifications, however there is a deeper meaning behind these two personality types. Each type of person is unique in their own way and make up their personality and how they deliver themselves. The typical stereotype is that introverts are the ones who tends to be more laidback and quieter than extroverts. This is often due to introverts thinking and reflecting on situations and issues before they speak or before they put ideas into actions. To better lead these individuals, it is important to allow them to think before they speak, give them time to reflect on ideas or solutions, and listen to them because they are the ones who often have the ideas backed by a though process.

An extrovert is the complete opposite. Extroverts tend to speak aloud when ideas or thoughts come to them. They tend to be outgoing, make quick decisions, and perform well in team-oriented situations and projects. Leading these individuals will be different. Understand that these individuals will want to jump right into conversation or problem solving. They prefer to multitask and speak as words come to them without much thought. Managing these individuals should be done by encouraging their enthusiasm that they often strive from.

There are also some people who do fall in between both these classifications depending on the scenario or environment they are in. I, for one, am more of an introvert. I do, however, bounce back and forth between these two classifications depending on the people I am with or the environment I am in. People will typically fall onto more of one side of the spectrum. Being able to determine which spectrum you fall into most is important for being able to effectively communicate to others. As an introvert, you may be more into closing your office door to escape people and concentrate on projects. If this is you, you must understand that employees may view this as if you are trying to shut them out. It is recommended to always leave the door open unless you have an important meeting, conversation, or project that others should not know about. Making this a habit and routine will allow team members to know when they can and cannot approach you. If the door is always closed, you are giving them no opportunity to know when you are available when needed and therefore, an absent manager.

Extroverts on the other hand are typically very outgoing individuals who spend a lot of time talking and socializing. This is very helpful when trying to make a name for yourself, because extroverts are more likely to greet everyone in the hall and be easy to approach. A downside of this is that they can be distracted by socializing too much and not focused on their work. Realizing you are an extrovert is important to be more cognizant about this trait and to be able to get work done in an effective manner.

As mentioned, multiple times, there is not a trait that is better to possess. Each presents its own unique qualities, good and bad, that make each workplace truly unique. There are many articles out there that suggest that extroverts make up most of the managerial world because of their personality. But introverts are more likely to succeed in situations that require more attention to details than social settings. Bill Gates and Warren Buffet, for example, are both highly successful businessmen and are introverts despite all the publicity and public gatherings they have encountered in their career. If you can identify your weaknesses and strengths, focusing on building your communication skills, given your classification of "introvert" or "extrovert", should help you excel in your career.

Aside from personality traits and types, there are also many employee types, which have their own personalities alone. There are four types of employees:

1. The Ambitious and Amiable- Innovative and eager to climb the professional ladder. Easy-going and smart. Hates Avoid conflicts.

2. Highly-functional Introvert- Quiet, but pleasant, individuals that provide stability. Hide their issues, which can cause discontent.

3. Anxious Warrior- Complains about the lack of time and workload. Will stay late to complete work. To best manage this personality type will require to understand what causes their anxiety.

4. Intense Temperament- These employees are most difficult to manage and can have sudden outburst over small issues. As a manager, it is important to understand what causes these issues as they can be preventable.

Listening makes up the second half of effective communication. It can come in two forms: passive and active. Passive listening occurs when what is being said is not being fully comprehended and can be interpreted as a type of "white noise". Active listening occurs when the listener is engaged into a conversation and interactive with the speaker. Managers are always expected to exhibit active listening skills.

One of the largest complaints employees have of their managers is that they are passive listeners. Have you ever had a manager or supervisor that no matter the importance of the subject that they seem disinterested or occupied doing something else? For those of you who have never had this happen, imagine going to your boss about an important project that you think would save the company thousands of dollars. You would expect them to be all over the idea. Instead, you get a manager who is tucked behind his laptop and you can see his eyes go side to side like a typewriter as he is reading an email while you are bringing up this idea. He then says, "mhmm, that sounds great, thank you for bringing that to my attention". Weeks go by without another word about this encounter and you think to yourself, "was he even listening to me?". A passive listener is very difficult to have as a manager and even a coworker because no matter what you say, they do not place importance on your encounter and therefore will result in a breakdown of communication that could lead to dissatisfaction or errors in the workplace.

As a manager, it is important to understand the differences between active and passive listening. Look back at your past conversations you have had with your spouse, your coworkers, your boss, etc., and then evaluate yourself. Did you play with a paperclip the entire time? Were you skimming emails or texting? Did you keep looking at your watch praying that the conversation would end? If so, STOP! This is not only important for those you communicate with but also for yourself.

Employers look for those who are engaged into their conversations and during interviews. Would you hire someone who was well qualified but seemed uninterested in the job and company, or rather someone who was underqualified but seemed excited in the opportunity and kept the conversation going? Most likely you would choose someone who seemed excited about the opportunity even if they were underqualified. Every conservation should be an engaged conversation.

These traits cannot be changed overnight. Therefore, it is important to realize what type of personality trait you possess and what type of listener you are during each encounter you have with someone. This should be done with different people in your personal and professional life. Paying special attention to the weaknesses you have in your listening skills will open your eyes about the listener you are and how each encounter may be different depending on who you communicate with. I promise you the more you can recognize your flaws and improve upon them, it will open more opportunities for you professionally with your coworkers and employees. Evaluating yourself on any level is important, for what I call: Personal Professional Quality Improvement. Using a PPQI will be discussed further in the next chapter.

MANAGEMENT FROM THE OUTSIDE

"Communicate unto the other person that which you would want him to communicate unto you if your positions were reversed"

-Aaron Goldman, Author of *Everything I Know About Marketing I Learned from Google*

Chapter Eight: Responsibilities

Being a manager requires a large amount of responsibility. In simplest form, responsibility is having control over people or things and being held accountable for their actions and outcomes. In a professional world, many things can go wrong. All it takes is one employee to cause the destruction of not only a relationship with a customer but can also damage the company's reputation. You may still be a leader, but as a manager you are in the driver's seat. Your actions can drive your team towards success, or you can be the reason they crash and burn.

Responsibilities of a manager can vary greatly depending on the industry. However, there are many responsibilities that align with each other. These basic responsibilities include:

- Ensuring the safety and health of the workers

- Developing a successful workforce

- Meeting goals and objectives

- Staff schedule and payroll

- Delegation

- Providing oversight and direction to workers

These responsibilities are very basic and adhere to practically any management job. These should be utilized in specific format in job descriptions based on the industry standards. An example of a job description that utilizes these responsibilities but makes them more geared towards a specific industry is as followed:

Job Title: Radiology Department Manager

Job Brief- The goal is for the Radiology Department Manager to oversee staff, and to provide the knowledge and expertise to drive the department towards operational and financial success.

Responsibilities include but not limited to:

- Oversee the day-to-day operations for both outpatients and inpatients

- Strategize and optimize department expenses

- Set and revise policies and procedures as appropriate

- Ensure HIPAA compliance through PACS, EMR, and daily practices

- Actively engaged in employee performance and yearly evaluations

- Optimize employee and patient satisfaction

- Provide the necessary documentation to regulatory agencies such as JCAHO, CMS, and AMAP

Requirements:

- ARRT certification required

- Certifications in at least two modalities preferred

- At least 2+ years as a manager

- Bachelor's degree in either business or medical imaging

As you can see, the above job description is more in depth than a general managerial position. This holds true on any job posting or description. You need to specify and outline the exact requirements that are expected of the position. Aside from outlining the requirements, it can also hold the user accountable for their performance. A worker who is not told from the beginning what is expected of them and outlining their responsibilities from the beginning can lead to many issues down the road. Getting this right from the start is important for future success.

Setting your department up for success starts with outlying important responsibilities on both a managerial and staff level. Responsibilities are very important because it sets the tone and expectations. Many positions and job descriptions are very generic and do not truly define what to expect in the given position. This automatically sets the candidate up for failure because they may be hired into a position that they were not expecting certain responsibilities. This leads to many issues such as dissatisfaction, unmanageable workload, and increased turnover.

Imagine you are the accounting manager of a large non-profit charitable organization. If you have a team of accountants that you trust, you may not micromanage their work and expect them to be honest and work with little to no supervision. Your lack of oversight of these employees allows one dishonest employee to falsify their statements from funding received by the government. This may have been something that they have been doing for the past two years, which allowed them to pocket $300,000 for themselves. For a large organization that handles millions of dollars a year from multiple contributors, it is very easy to funnel that kind of money if, as a manager, you are not holding your employees and yourself responsible for their actions. The moral of the story is that you, as the manager, are ultimately responsible for this employee and most likely you will be fired right alongside of the accountant. Because this is a non-profit organization that receives money from individuals and the government, this could be leaked to the media and people would be much less likely to contribute to a company that does dishonest business. This will hurt the company in the long run. As a manager it is very important to understand that you are more responsible for the actions of your workers then they are of themselves.

The responsibilities of a manager are endless and can vary in many different types of industries, but they can also be very similar in nature. If you look on Indeed and type in "manager", you can click on 5 different positions and you will notice very similar basic responsibilities along with industry-specific responsibilities. In many roles, a manager is usually responsible for planning, directing, and overseeing the operational and financial aspect of a business or department. With these responsibilities, duties of a manager require delegation, organization, and accountability.

Delegation is authorizing individuals to do certain duties often allowing those who are best qualified or able to perform them in a timely manner. This is different from dictating because delegation is authorizing individuals to do a specific job while dictating is forcing individuals to do tasks in an authoritative manner. Delegation is often the preferred method of ensuring tasks are being done by the proper individuals and gives employees a sense of authority and responsibility to achieve the task. Dictating is a negative form of assigning someone else to get a task completed.

If delegation does not work, then dictation may be necessary. When you have to start dictating responsibilities it can be a sign that an employee most likely has little respect for you or authority. Or it can be as simple as the employee feels uncomfortable to complete the task due to lack of training or unrealistic deadlines. As a manager it is your responsibility to ensure that the correct people take care of certain tasks and this requires you to understand your employee's capabilities to delegate them accordingly.

Another important responsibility of all managers is organization. Creating a group of individuals to work towards a common goal creates an organized workforce and sets clear objectives when things are organized. An organized department or office is the managers responsibility. Having a group of individuals not knowing what their role is can create many avoidable inefficiencies that are inevitable to occur. Having an organized department is just as important as being organized as a manager.

Being an organized manager starts with physically being organized. You simply cannot be a disorganized manager and run a department to its maximum potential and efficiency. Being organized requires creating yourself memos, reminders, and calendars so you do not miss the many meetings and deadlines that are to be met on a weekly basis. Decluttering your workspace to create a clean slate for every time you sit down will allow for you to do your job more effectively. An employee should never come to your office with you fumbling over a thousand pieces of paper while you try to find their performance appraisal. Nothing is more off putting than sitting in a manager's cluttered office seeing them fumble over files and loose papers. Set a good example and get organized. After you get yourself organized, you can then work on getting your department organized. Basic organization makes everything run more smoothly not only for yourself but also your organization.

Organization allows you to focus on the other aspects of managing that can be easily overlooked. Once you have yourself physically organized, you can focus your efforts on operational organization. Operational organization allows you to be able to look different aspects of how the department is run and eliminate inefficient workflows, redundancies, and disorganized work areas. Finding these inefficiencies is an important part of operational organization because it will allow work to be completed quicker, which opens the gates for more possibilities. When a manager can quantifiably increase efficiency, they are able to represent their talents on a higher level.

Accountability is also another large portion of the responsibilities of a manager. Not only do you need to hold others accountable for their actions but should have accountability for your own actions. Accountability is being able to stand by your decisions. As a manager, it is also your responsibility of holding others accountable for their decisions and actions.

Anything employees do, good or bad, will be a direct representation of the manager. Having a good mutual understanding with your employees is an important aspect to build a solid manager-employee relationship. Employees should know when they need to get approval and when they do not, or a bad decision may make the manager or company look bad. Not every decision needs to go through the manager, however there are many things that should if there is any doubt that the manager may not approve. Make this clear to employees so they are not subordinate to your expectations.

Observing your own accountability creates integrity. Owning up for your decisions is an important part of management. Throwing your staff under the bus for a mistake they made but are never held accountable for displays more of a lack of accountability of the manager, not the staff. The purpose of a manager is to be able to represent not only themselves but the actions of their staff. How the department is running directly reflects on the manager and they should, therefore, be expected to have high accountability in their managerial position.

Responsibilities can be endless for a manager. Some managers work on the floor alongside staff, some have administrative duties, and others do both. Company size and depending on the industry, these responsibilities vary greatly. A great way for managers to understand if they are successfully completing their responsibilities would require manager's holding themselves accountable utilizing a Personal Quality Assurance tool, which will be discussed further in the next chapter.

"Success on any major scale requires you to accept responsibility…. In the final analysis, the one quality that all successful people have is the ability to take on responsibility."

- Michael Korda, Editor-in-Chief of Simon & Schuster.

Chapter Nine: Personal Quality Assurance

There are many branches of quality management such as quality improvement, quality control, and quality assurance. All three of these branches of quality management focuses on producing products or services with minimal errors or flaws. Quality management is such an important role that it is not unheard of making more than six figures as a quality manager. These managers are responsible for finding flaws, making improvements, and increasing efficiency as much as possible that can save companies millions of dollars in the long run.

Most quality managers utilize tools such as Six Sigma, Lean, Total Quality Management, and PDSA models to successfully do their job. Knowing each one of these models is important for any type of manager to understand at least the general idea and theory of. Each model is slightly different but aimed at achieving the same goal, which is to improve quality.

Quality improvement focuses on measurable data that incorporates the processes and systems that are in place to produce a given product or system. Quality improvement utilizes a PDSA model, which stands for Plan-Do-Study-Act, which is defined below:

Plan- Identify an opportunity and plan to make a change.

Do- Implement the idea temporarily. Scale it small that makes it easy to manage during early stages.

Study- Analyze the data and compare to the data prior to implementation.

Act- If there was a positive change, implement it on a wider scale and continuously gather results. Make changes if necessary.

Quality control has more focus on establishing the best standards or processes, typically formatted in a flowchart or diagram. It relies on active participation from both managers and employees to create environments that will produce the best outcomes. If employees do not follow the flowchart or diagrams that are created, the process does not work, and errors will occur. It is the manager's duty to ensure that employees are following the flowcharts and diagrams that are created. Overseeing the workflow gives managers a better sense of any breakdowns in the process and allows them to adjust any portion as necessary. It also creates consistencies and sets guidelines for smoother operation.

Quality assurance on the other hand typically is used in ensuring that processes are being delivered with little to no flaws. This one relies heavily on workers since there are multiple stages of producing any type of product or service. Quality assurance has a strong focus on minimizing mistakes, which often come from human error. The initial stages of developing a workflow is important for the manager to worry about because it will create a smoother system to set employees up for success. Early development is important during this type of quality management and is important to gather quality assurance data to make a difference such as Profiles Performance Indicators.

Profiles Performance Indicators (PPI) utilizes individual's job performance and personality utilizing DISC analysis. DISC analysis breaks users into four different segments: Dominate, Influential, Steady, and Compliant. Utilizing the PPI can be a very valuable business tool that evaluates both the performance of employees and is also great for motivation. It allows managers to better understand their employees on a personal level to understand how they work. This will allow the manager to be able to utilize employees in a more efficient manner based on their PPI. However, this tool is only as valuable as the user makes it. If this will be used for a simple yearly appraisal, then it is not being used for its maximum benefit and should therefore not be utilized.

With all these quality tools, there are none that evaluates managers and employees on a professional level. Although this is not an official tool of quality assurance, we will call this type of quality management tool "personal quality assurance". Personal quality assurance should be a new measurement that evaluates individuals and their performance to complete quality work. Yes, this may sound like an evaluation that you may get once or twice a year. However, this type of quality management would take a deeper dive into your typical yearly evaluation.

Typical workplace evaluations can include a variety of measurements depending on the type of workplace or field you are in. These can range from sales goals, frequency in which you practice hand hygiene, call outs, poor reviews, good reviews, and so on. And let us be frank. Does your manager even notice these, or do they just mark what they please? Chances are you have encountered a few managers who do not take these evaluations seriously and occasionally some that will.

What if the tables are turned and instead of the manager evaluating the employees, the employees evaluate the manager? Yes, this does exist, but what is done with this information? These evaluations typically consist of a few questions that ask what they are doing well and what they can do better, and it then gets filed away where it will never be looked at again. As a manager it is important to receive anonymous constructive feedback from your employees. Hold yourself accountable for your goals, your employee's morale, and constantly challenge the position in which you hold. Allow employees to look over your job description and have them circle areas that they think needs improvement on your end. Ask for feedback on the evaluation itself. Let your guard down and let your employees be as honest as possible. This is the only way of having personal quality assurance because you may believe you are doing all the right things while the employees you manage are not seeing eye to eye with you. Setting personal quality goals for yourself will not only make you a better manager who is well liked but will also allow you to self-improve and excel professionally.

Traditionally speaking, quality control is fed off quality assurance and quality management. You cannot have control without having the other two established first. Throwing personal quality assurance in the mix will provide a form of checks and balances to ensure that all four of these concepts are being utilized in unison.

When you are focused too much on the process, you lose focus of the product. When you focus too much time on one or two aspects of the big picture, the focus is shifted away from focusing on all the aspects. This may not cause an immediate issue but is not viable for long-term success. Treat each one of these individually as they are all an important process for success. There are many books and articles about quality assurance, quality control, and quality management and most likely you already have some responsibilities in those realms to begin with. Because there are many resources on those three topics, let us focus more on the personal quality assurance, which brings those three together.

Personal quality assurance will hold yourself accountable for ensuring you are carrying out the three factors of quality. Setting up standards for yourself and adhering to those standards are only a fraction of what PQA is all about. PQA will help understand what you are doing right and what you are doing wrong. It will bring to light on how you can personally improve on your actions and not only grow yourself as a professional but also bring out desired results.

Employees typically get feedback on their performance or mistakes while managers rarely get that in return. This is a way of setting professional standards and giving accountability for yourself and your position. If everyone rates you low on communication, then make that your goal to improve upon that following year. As a manager you need to have a scale to not only evaluate yourself but have others evaluate your performance as well. The scales that are listed below can be for not only yourself but also those whom you manage. They can be measurable and comparable year to year, while the comment section will help create a channel of open and honest feedback that may not otherwise be given. Below we can see how the evaluation can be of importance towards personal quality assurance by showing the areas that they should be focusing on for the following year. The questions should be short and straightforward to easy evaluation.

Manager is actively engaged in continuous process improvements   1 2 3 4 5

    Comments:

Manager is actively engaged in continuous product/service improvements   1 2 3 4 5

    Comments:

Manager made significant positive changes since past year
                1 2 3 4 5

    Comments:

Manager encouraged others to share ideas and put them into action   1 2 3 4 5

    Comments:

Manager provides valuable feedback and support throughout projects   1 2 3 4 5

    Comments:

Manager holds others and him/herself accountable for their actions   1 2 3 4 5

    Comments:

    The above is a very simple grading scale that managers can use on themselves. Employees will feel important in providing honest feedback for the manager to improve upon him or herself, which should, in return, directly affect their performance in the long run. For PQA to work, managers must invest their time and effort to take these evaluations seriously and to work upon their weakest grades. If a manager scores a 2 on the section of providing valuable feedback and support, their goal in the upcoming months should be focused on providing others with feedback and support. How does this help quality, you may ask? When employees are provided with feedback, they not only get guidance, they also gain reassurance that their manager cares and is invested in their work.

Assessing yourself is equally as important for comparison. If you graded yourself a 4 in the section of providing feedback and support while others graded yourself an average of 2, there are clearly some discrepancies that need addressed. If you plan on filing your evaluations without truly evaluating and comparing them, you might as well not go through with the process of evaluations to begin with. This whole process starts with you and what you will make of it. Employees respect a manager who wants to learn about their weaknesses and physically acts on them by improving on their weaknesses. It shows the commitment and lengths a manager will take to take accountability for the long-term success of the company.

The biggest take on this is that as a manager, you should create an atmosphere where feedback should be open in both directions. It should never be viewed as a negative concept but rather an empowering one where both managers and employees are able to create a sense of trust and be able to grow professionally together. However, there should be limits on openness that will be discussed in the last chapter.

"We all need people who will give us feedback. That's how we improve."

- Bill Gates, Founder of Microsoft Corporation

Chapter Ten: Social Media & Appreciation

Social media and appreciation are two separate topics that I will not provide enough information to make up their own chapter alone, but I feel is important to discuss. Social media is a topic that is often ignored when it comes to management and I am not sure why. Maybe because it is so new that writers or researchers have not done much research on it, or perhaps we are just blind and naive that social media affects management. Social media can be a very valuable tool in management, or it can be disastrous. As with many decisions you make in life, the outcomes can be controlled solely on your own actions.

Although Friendster came before Myspace, Myspace kicked off the social media frenzy in 2003 that had many platforms following suite shortly thereafter. There are many social media platforms that came after Myspace, such as Facebook, Instagram, Twitter, YouTube, Tinder, Match.com, and many more. I will refer to these as recreational social media. Then you have more professional social media platforms such as LinkedIn that allows you to connect and interact with other professionals and can be used for job searching purposes. There is also Meetup that can connect you with like-minded people in your area to discuss a variety of business and professional topics in person. I will refer to these as professional social media platforms.

As a manager you must be very careful in how you utilize the above platforms. Can you be a CEO of a Fortune 500 company and still have a Facebook? Absolutely. Can you be a CEO of a Fortune 500 company and make comments that may come off as racist towards an ethnic group? Yes, you can. However, do not expect yourself to be working there for much longer. Because social media is so connected, your family is also under the same scrutiny when you are in a high position within a well-known company. A daughter of a CEO posted racial comments online and the company was under fire with boycotts and bad publicity. Although this is an extreme circumstance, freedom of speech is protected by the first amendment but does not mean you are protected from your job. Whether the post or comment was racist, threatening, homophobic, etc. you can almost guarantee that someone will screenshot it and will have hard evidence against you. Nothing posted is ever truly private.

Using social media as a working professional can be tricky. There is a perception that managers should create bonds and trust with their employees by developing personal connections. Yet there is another side that says work relationships should stay at work and to keep personal lives separate. No matter which side you are on, the biggest take on this is if you use common sense there should be no issues. This is easier said than done for some people, especially if a topic hits a wrong nerve or feels like a personal attack against them. These attacks happen often with employees posting how they hate their job or boss.

Every situation is unique on whether it is appropriate to add or accept your employees to your recreational social media sites. If you worked your way into a management role and made friends along the way as co-workers, then most likely you have a few people on your friends list that are now working under your supervision.

These people have already made the cut onto your friends list before you became manager. The question now is, do you delete them and start declining all future requests, or do you keep them and accept future requests but limit what they can see? Again, it all depends, but it is something to think about and consider.

Although social media creates a sense of connection sharing baby announcements, birthday celebrations, etc. between a manager and employee, you also do not want to be put into an awkward situation where something inappropriate was posted. I would recommend taking any photos from the account and save them onto your hard drive or thumb drive. Then deactivate the account and start a new one and add only close family and friends. Let us be honest, how many of your "friends" have you talked to in the past five years? Probably less than 10% of them. If you do decide to allow a recreational social-media friendship, as a manager, be sure to:

- Never be the first to request the friendship.

- Be careful of what you post.

    o Do not post political views.

    o Avoid sharing controversial topics.

    o Never talk poorly towards anyone or their opinions.

- Be careful of your past posts and tagged photos. With that being said...you should probably take that picture that your best man took of you passed out at your bachelor party 10 years ago.

- If you are questioning if you should post something, you probably should not post it.

Professional social media, however, can be a very valuable tool for both parties. As a manager, you want to create a sense of credibility by building a nice portfolio and listing all certifications, volunteer work, and more that employees may not know about you. Many of times we have managers who you may not think are qualified to lead a team and lack the necessary skillsets of their job. Showcasing that you are a Six Sigma Master Black Belt with an MBA and have increased customer satisfaction scores by 75% allows employees to get a better visual and level of respect for your accomplishments. On the other end, employees can do the same thing. They can showcase their goals and accomplishments to the manager, which may not have been known about otherwise.

In my non-supervisory role, I posted on LinkedIn about completing my MBA and was reached out to by a director that I have encountered a few times, but they never knew I was interested in management until they saw my post. This showcased my interest to those who may turn into mentors or advocates for me to advance my career. This type of method allows you to brag about your accomplishments and to be recognized by the right people with a simple post or update in your profile.

One issue with professional social media platforms is that these can be used for recruitment purposes and finding out an employee is looking for a job can lead to some issues in the workplace. Depending on the state in which you work, either the manager or employee can be fired for simply looking for another job. These are called "at-will employment states" and can fire you for any reason. This leaves the user in a difficult spot. You may look for or be open to new opportunities, however you cannot remain completely confidential when using these platforms. It is an unfortunate reality that you try to look for your best interest but may get fired in return. These workplaces exist and if they will fire you for being open to new opportunities than you are better off anyways. Employers that do not support their employee's growth are not worth working for.

Many social media platforms have settings where you can change who is allowed to see certain photos or post. Use this with caution as whatever is posted to the internet can always be traced or screenshotted from someone else. One wrong comment or post can land you out of a job or even in legal trouble. I cannot emphasize enough that nothing is ever truly private online. These last few paragraphs are not meant to scare you or to have you delete all your accounts because the lack of social media, on the other hand, can come off as odd or you can come off as someone that is hiding something.

With social media surrounding constantly surrounding the majority of us, if you choose not to have a Facebook, Twitter, or Instagram, I do recommend at least making a LinkedIn with a professional photograph. Having a professional photograph makes your site more credible and recruiters will be able to put a face to the name. I think we have a good understanding of the use of social media and the "dos and don'ts" surrounding it. Let us move on to the last topic of this chapter and book, which is appreciation.

MANAGEMENT FROM THE OUTSIDE

Appreciation plays a large factor in high-morale workplaces. Appreciation can come in many forms as it can be a simple gesture, a monetary bonus, and anything in between. Great managers try to understand their employees' individual needs to best show their appreciation in a personalized manner. It would be too easy to just start paying employees more, giving them better benefits, and giving them unlimited autonomy, and we all know that being a manager is not always easy. This type of appreciation is not sustainable for long-term success.

Simple gestures can come from developing personal connections with your employees by understanding what their needs, wants, and motivators are that can help you be creative in how you deliver your appreciation. An employee that tends to be shy and reserved may hate to be nominated for employee of the month in front of a large group of people. These types of employees may benefit from a gift card to their favorite restaurant that you just learned about because you took the time to get to know them. Not only does the gift card resemble a physical form of monetary appreciation but also an emotional appreciation that the manager was actively listening by getting a gift card to their favorite restaurant.

Use a raffle-reward system. Give employees that achieve goals, meet deadlines, work extra, or get positive comments from patients or customers a raffle ticket. Keep these tickets in a locked box and draw one ticket every month. Have prizes such as a personal day off, a tablet, Yeti tumbler, or anything else that fits your budget. Get even more crazy and do a yearly raffle for a large prize such as a week off, a large bonus, an all-expenses paid vacation, or anything in between. This can be a random drawing of all the raffles gathered in the year or whoever has the most. Be creative with this as every place will have different budgets and allowances.

Google LLC provides their employees with onsite medical care, excellent death benefits that ensures financial coverage for the family, and generous parental care. They also focus on promoting a creative workplace where employees can bring their pets to work and the employees can enjoy every meal for free at their cafeteria. However, not every company is able to provide their employees with these types of perks. Focusing on your employee's needs and developing environments that are suited around those needs can create a significant boost in morale. High morale equals higher job satisfaction, which leads to higher performance.

Psychologist, William James, has been quoted saying, "the deepest principle in human nature is the craving to be appreciated". What this means is that appreciation is truly a human need and those needs should be met in any aspect of your life, whether it be personal or in the workplace. Recently you may have been doing extra chores around the house or going above and beyond at work. You may be doing this out of the kindness of your heart, or possibly returning the appreciation towards your significant other by doing extra chores, or maybe you were off for a week at work and wanted to "make it up" to your fellow employees. It is completely normal to do extra or work harder without any external motivators or incentives.

Doing more than required does not work well if you continue this habit long term with the expectation that you will be appreciated for your efforts without ever being acknowledged. The same would be true for your employees. They will not continue going beyond the call of duty if they never get appreciation in return. Without any praise or appreciation for doing extra for multiple times in a row or weeks at a time, you may be less reluctant to do extra in the future. Why would an employee continue going above and beyond in their work if there are no external motivators for them such as being promoted, increase in pay, or even a simple act of recognition?

Abraham Maslow was a psychologist who developed a pyramid of human needs that needed to be accomplished to motivate individuals to feel fulfilled. Most of you reading this have heard about this theory repeatedly throughout your education, but for those who have not, or as a refresher. Maslow's hierarchy of needs started at the basic level of physiological needs that consisted of water, food, air, and shelter. The next step is safety such as personal security, followed by love and belonging. The next step is esteem, which is having respect, recognition, and autonomy. Self-actualization is the last tier that focuses on the desire to become the most one can be and achieve. These can be very generic and pertain to multiple scenarios but is broken down below in Figure 9.1 that focuses on needs in the workplace to achieve ultimate success.

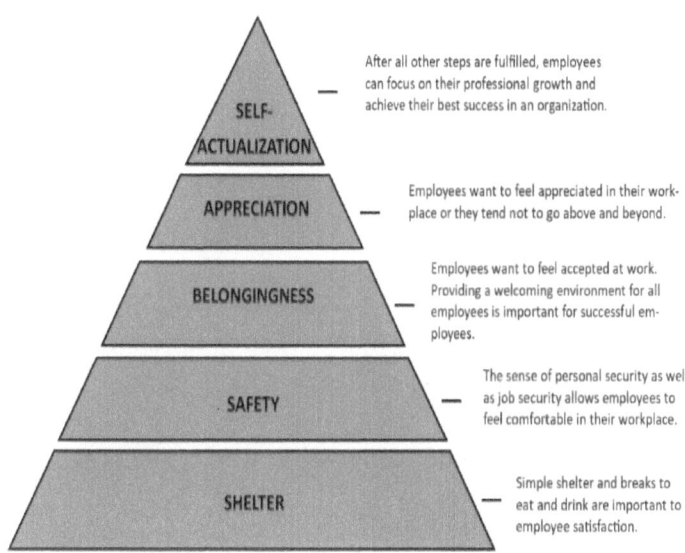

Figure 9.1 Workplace hierarchy of needs

An article by *Harvard Business Review* mentions that the feeling that we truly matter is by knowing that we are contributing a unique value and being recognized for it. They also included a study conducted by Towers Watson, who performed a worldwide study, that showed that the highest driver of engagement was the feeling that their managers were genuinely interested in their wellbeing and only 40% of workers actually felt that way. When employees start feeling their energy is wasted, they stop trying. Satisfied employees may not be engaged, but engaged employees are often satisfied. As a manager, it is very important to evaluate if, and how, you are showing your appreciation to your employees to avoid employees feeling this way. Simple solutions can include but not limited to:

- Send "Thank You" cards.

- Verbally tell employees they are doing a good job, when they truly are, do not make it a habit just to say it.

- Having parties/lunch when your team achieves goals and milestones.

- Make announcements on the company website or send a mass email of a big accomplishment such as someone getting a degree, passing a certification, or welcoming new team members.

- Keep staff posted on any educational opportunities that they may be interested in. This shows that you are invested in their future and interests.

- Promoting within and sharing any other opportunities that may interest your employees.

- Give personalized gifts around the holidays.

- Create incentive programs where employees can earn rewards for their performance.

- During employee evaluations have them fill out a card that ask questions about their goals, interests, likes and dislikes, and use those to your advantage.

- On occasion, depending on what type of field you work in, it may be acceptable to invite a team member for lunch. This should be done carefully and with more than one employee at the same time to keep your intentions harmless.

As a manager, employees expect you to know about what they do on a daily basis. You may be an office manager that oversees multiple departments such as accounting, human resources, and sales. Just because you may not be a certified public accountant does not mean you cannot understand or witness their workflow, challenges, and achievements. Shadowing and/or performing the duties of each employee, if feasible, at least once a day per year is important in understanding and appreciating their contributions they provide for the business. It may be difficult when you are responsible for more than twenty employees. You can cut down this theory by only doing half a day, but it is only as valuable as you make it. It should be done in a non-micromanaging way and have employees know you are there to understand their roles to make necessary changes to help better their workplace experience.

Appreciation should be given whenever there is an opportunity to, which is more than you may realize. Although you should reward and appreciate everyone who excels, it is also important to focus on those who do not.

MANAGEMENT FROM THE OUTSIDE

Focusing your attention to those who may be lacking in performance may be from you not giving them the attention that they once needed. If this does not work, then there may be some other underlying problem going on. Using your best judgement and evaluating your current practices of appreciation is the best step to start appreciating your employees more than you did before.

Being an engaged manager will allow you to notice more and provide the necessary support needed for your team members. You will start recognizing their efforts more, see new opportunities, and be more readily available to those that need you. Be engaged, communicate, and be a good leader and you are on the right track on becoming a better manager.

"Clients do not come first. Employees come first. If you take care of your employees, they will take care of the clients."

-Richard Branson, Founder of the Virgin Group

Epilogue/Conclusion

Although this book contains facts and proven strategies, it is far from a scholarly resource or to be used as a professional source of information. However, I do hope that by the time you close this book that you have gained some form of motivation, ideas, or knowledge that will be beneficial to make yourself a better manager and leader than before you opened the first page.

There may be some points or chapters that you disagree with and that is okay. What creates great leaders and managers are disagreements and challenging certain practices or methodologies and to choose the best one that is most practical for them or their department. My biggest goal was to be able to connect with some of you, and to either give developing managers a new perspective to think about as they are developing into their professional roles or to bring managers who may be stuck in a rut to view how management is viewed from the outside looking in.

MANAGEMENT FROM THE OUTSIDE

Acknowledgments

This book was written based on many experiences and encounters. This could not have been possible without those who I have come across in my life. Although I have encountered dozens of individuals who have influenced or shaped me in one way or another, I apologize for anyone that I leave out. I want all my friends, family members, managers, and coworkers to know that they all shaped who I have become, what I have accomplished, and what I will accomplish in the future.

It is safe to say that my parents and sister have influenced the majority of who I am today. They have always supported my decisions and held me responsible for them, whether it was buying a car, going to college versus community college, moving to New Jersey and North Carolina, and any other decision I have made in between. If I wanted something, I were to work for it. I cannot appreciate this style of parenting because it gave me the work ethic I have today, and I am forever grateful that they made me work for what I have.

Adam, my roommate in college was a huge influence on my studies and encouraged me to keep trying after I hit a few roadblocks academically. He recently graduated with a PhD in Neuroscience and this put a lot of pressure on me living with someone so academically inclined. I never once felt belittled for our academic differences and that makes all the difference.

While I attended my clinicals, my teacher at the time was in school, working as a clinical instructor, and working in radiology. More than halfway through the program he was offered a job as a radiology manager and hired me after graduation. He showed me the potential and opportunities that a career in radiology has to offer. Although he does not know it, his desire to move up and his management style is what made me interested in becoming a radiology manager. Thank you, Ron.

Lastly, Jess, my wife has always been uncertain with my sporadic decision making. In the end, she knows how stubborn I am and supports me through all my decisions I make. She sacrificed time and had lots of patience when I had to make school a priority for two years, and also the attention I have spent on book. Thank you for being you, I love you.

About the Author

Zachary Frace grew up in the Allentown, Pennsylvania region and had a normal life growing up with both his parents and sister. He played and enjoyed sports growing up. In high school, Zach suffered a concussion during a football game. He went to an urgent care where they performed x-rays of the cervical spine. After looking at the x-rays a lightbulb lit up that this is could be the career that he has been frantically searching for. After he researched radiography careers and programs, he ended up attending Bloomsburg University of Pennsylvania for two years and then attended clinicals for another two years in Jersey City, New Jersey at CarePoint Health School of Radiography. Since radiology technologist do not get paid in clinicals he bartended and was the manager at a restaurant in Hoboken, which sparked an interest in management. He graduated with a bachelor's degree in Medical Imaging, passed his boards and was offered a position at his clinical site, Bayonne Medical Center all in the same month.

After graduation, he realized the endless opportunities that the field of radiology has to offer. Being the ambitious person he is, he searched for the next step. This search lead him to getting certified a year later in CT Scan, which allowed him to be more marketable and to get out of the Jersey City area back home with family in Pennsylvania. Unfortunately, this move was short lived due to some issues and had to resort to a new plan. He found an opportunity for both himself and his fiancée, at the time, in a well-known vacation destination in North Carolina, called The Outer Banks.

The entire year of 2017 consisted of moving, getting acclimated to the area, and getting married. However, Zach was still looking for the next step and that was to go back to school to get his MBA with a concentration in Healthcare Administration. He was able to find an online program allowing him to work fulltime and able to complete in two years. During those two years he got involved in many aspects of his workplace. He took on inventory management, staff scheduling, radiology representative in stroke-ready certification, submitted a project for a Board Quality Award, improved code-stroke workflows and efficiencies, and also became a superuser for EHR, PACS, CT scan and X-ray. He also got certified in Executive Management, Project Management-Lean Process, and Six Sigma Green Belt. However, after graduating that still was not enough. He decided to create a management blog and write this book, not because he is an expert in management and leadership but because if there is any piece of information that can help someone in their life or career, then time is not wasted. Now, what is the next thing he can dive into?

www.ingramcontent.com/pod-product-compliance
Lightning Source LLC
Chambersburg PA
CBHW030714220526
45463CB00005B/2038